THE
GOSPEL
FOR LIFE

—— SERIES ——

THE GOSPEL &

Parenting

Also in the *Gospel for Life* series

THE
GOSPEL
FOR LIFE

— SERIES —

THE GOSPEL &

Parenting

SERIES EDITORS

RUSSELL MOORE *and*
ANDREW T. WALKER

B&H
PUBLISHING GROUP
NASHVILLE, TENNESSEE

978-1-4336-9044-0

Published by B&H Publishing Group
Nashville, Tennessee

Dewey Decimal Classification: 649
Subject Heading: PARENTING \ BIBLE. N.T. GOSPELS \
CHILD REARING

1 2 3 4 5 6 7 8 • 21 20 19 18 17

CONTENTS

Series Preface

Russell Moore

Why Should the *Gospel for Life* Series Matter to Churches?

IN ACTS CHAPTER 2, WE READ ABOUT THE DAY OF PENTECOST, the day when the resurrected Lord Jesus Christ sent the Holy Spirit from heaven onto His church. The Day of Pentecost was a spectacular day—there were manifestations of fire, languages being spoken by people who didn't know them, and thousands of unbelievers coming to faith in this recently resurrected Messiah. Reading this passage, we go from account to account of heavenly shock and awe, and yet the passage ends in an unexpectedly simple way: "And they devoted themselves to the apostles' teaching and the fellowship, to the breaking of bread and the prayers" (Acts 2:42 ESV).

I believe one thing the Holy Spirit wants us to understand from this is that these "ordinary" things are not less spectacular than what preceded them—in fact, they may be more so. The disciplines of discipleship, fellowship, community, and prayer are the signs that tell us the kingdom of Christ is here. That means that for Christians, the most crucial moments in our walk with Jesus Christ don't happen in the thrill of "spiritual highs." They happen in the common hum of everyday life in quiet, faithful obedience to Christ.

That's what the *Gospel for Life* series is about: taking the truths of Scripture, the story of our redemption and adoption by a risen Lord Jesus, and applying them to the questions and situations that we all face in the ordinary course of life.

Our hope is that churches will not merely find these books interesting, but also helpful. The *Gospel for Life* series is meant to assist pastors and church leaders to answer urgent questions that people are asking, questions that the church isn't always immediately ready to answer. Whether in a counseling session or alongside a sermon series, these books are intended to come alongside church leaders in discipling members to see their lives with a Kingdom mentality.

Believers don't live the Christian life in isolation but rather as part of a gospel community, the church. That's why we have structured the *Gospel for Life* series to be easily utilized in anything from a small group study context to a new member or new believer class. None of us can live worthy of the gospel by ourselves, and thankfully, none have to.

Why are we so preoccupied with the idea of living life by and through the gospel? The answer is actually quite simple: Because the gospel changes everything. The gospel isn't a mere theological system or a political idea, though it shapes both our theology and our politics. The gospel is the Good News that there is a Kingdom far above and beyond the borders of this world, where death is dead and sin and sorrow cease. The gospel is about how God brings this Kingdom to us by reconciling us to Himself through Christ.

That means two things. First, it means the gospel fulfills the hopes that our idols have promised and betrayed. The Scripture says that all God's promises are yes in Jesus (2 Cor. 1:20). As sinful human beings, we all tend to think what we really want is freedom from authority, inheritance without obedience like the prodigal son. But what Jesus offers is the authority we were designed to live under, an inheritance we by no means deserve to share, and the freedom that truly satisfies our souls.

Second, this means that the gospel isn't just the start of the Christian life but rather the vehicle that carries it along. The gospel is about the daily reality of living as an adopted child of a resurrected Father-King, whose Kingdom is here and is still coming. By looking at our jobs, our marriages, our families, our government, and the entire universe through a gospel lens, we live differently. We will work and marry and vote with a Kingdom mind-set, one that prioritizes the permanent things of

Christ above the fleeting pleasures of sin and the vaporous things of this world.

The *Gospel for Life* series is about helping Christians and churches navigate life in the Kingdom while we wait for the return of its King and its ultimate consummation. The stakes are high. To get the gospel wrong when it comes to marriage can lead to a generation's worth of confusion about what marriage even is. To get the gospel wrong on adoption can leave millions of "unwanted" children at the mercy of ruthless sex traffickers and callous abusers. There's no safe space in the universe where getting the gospel wrong will be merely an academic blunder. That's why these books exist—to help you and your church understand what the gospel is and what it means for life.

Theology doesn't just think; it walks, weeps, and bleeds. The *Gospel for Life* series is a resource intended to help Christians see their theology do just that. When you see all of life from the perspective of the Kingdom, everything changes. It's not just about miraculous moments or intense religious experiences. Our gospel is indeed miraculous, but as the disciples in Acts learned, it's also a gospel of the ordinary.

Introduction

Andrew T. Walker

IF YOU HAVE CHILDREN, IT'S NOT A QUESTION OF WHETHER they'll have a parent. It's a question of who will be the one doing the parenting. You? Or the surrounding culture?

To parent in a way that honors Christ requires active attention to the parenting task. What do I mean exactly? I mean that children don't become strong Christians and good citizens by accident. Like making disciples, it doesn't happen on accident. Parenting requires constant attention to a child's heart, directing him or her in the ways of the Lord.

Parenting is no easy task. As a young father myself, I wake up daily to the reality that it's my job not just to discipline the daughters God has given me, but to instruct them about how the world works, and how to function within it.

Parenting is a big task. And considering that it's a task that most every single person will at some point in their life take up, it's important that Christians understand how God designed parenting to work.

Because many people become a parent in their lifetime, we decided to dedicate a whole volume to the task of parenting. There are many other books out there on parenting, but we hope that this small, accessible volume will serve as an introduction to the very concept of what it means to be a Christian who parents their children *Christianly.*

How are we going to do this? We want to hit all of the points that we think it necessary to discuss parenting. Each book in the *Gospel for Life* series is structured the same: What are we for? What does the gospel say? How should the Christian live? How should the church engage? What does the culture say?

This book is not only for parents with children in their home right now. This book is for future parents, grandparents, and single friends who live in loving church communities that include parents in their fellowship. Oftentimes, those outside the business of parenting (especially those with small children) can be the best encouragers and counselors. This book is for you.

The Gospel & Parenting is intended to be an introductory look at how Christians should engage parenting from every angle of the Christian's life—their place in culture, their engagement as everyday Christians, and their role in the body of Christ—the church. We want no stone unturned when talking about how the gospel of Jesus Christ shapes us as a people on mission for God in every sphere of our life.

CHAPTER

1

What Are We For?

Randy Stinson

IN NOVEMBER OF 2004 MY WIFE AND I WERE IN AN EARTH-quake in Taipei, Taiwan. It was a first for us and, thankfully, the epicenter was far enough into the Pacific Ocean that there was very little damage. While that experience was disconcerting enough, it was the multiple aftershocks that we experienced over the next few days that really gave us pause. It wasn't just the after-shocks; it was the way that the natives of Taipei responded. With thousands of people walking in the street, the tremor would hit, and nearly everyone kept walking as if nothing had happened.

Hardly anyone looked up to see if anything was falling. Hardly anyone stopped to even see what the response of others might be. Apparently something that is supposed to be a bone-jarring event can become so commonplace that it doesn't even get a response. I don't think you're supposed to be able to get used to the ground shaking beneath your feet.

But that's exactly what happened.

This is what often happens with regard to parenting in Christian circles. The air we breathe in an increasingly secularized culture can create an environment where we become accustomed to unbiblical philosophies that undermine our biblical worldview. Sometimes Christian parents want so desperately to be their child's friend that they minimize discipline and boundaries. Their priority is for their child to like them and they end up losing the respect of the child.

On the other end of the spectrum, sometimes Christian parents are overly focused on authority to such a degree that they end up relating to their children through fear and intimidation. They tend to micromanage their child so that they can exert complete control and they end up creating resentment in the child.

Still other Christian parents become overly preoccupied with performance and external behavior. This focus often leads the child to believe that in order to be loved, they have to perform and that their parents' love is conditional.

In order to avoid these and other unbiblical notions of parenting, the gospel must not only be brought to bear on the task of parenting, it must be at the heart. Christian parenting should be rooted in the gospel of Jesus Christ, and it is in this light that evangelicals must affirm certain things in order to ensure that their parenting meets this goal.

The Primacy of Scripture

First, evangelicals affirm the primacy of Scripture. In many ways, this might be considered a given. But when it comes to parenting, evangelicals often do not turn to the Scriptures first. More often they simply default to the parenting strategy embraced by their own parents. Or they will simply embrace the philosophy of their peers. This is partially because many evangelicals actually do not believe the Bible has much to say about parenting at all. They know that there are some Proverbs that are written from a father to his son. They know that Colossians admonishes fathers to not exasperate their children, and of course Ephesians exhorts children to obey their parents. Many evangelicals conclude then, that since there are very few places that explicitly address parents or children, the Bible has very little to say about the subject.

However, Paul told Timothy that "all Scripture is inspired by God and is profitable for teaching, for rebuking, for correcting, for training in righteousness" (2 Tim. 3:16), which means that the whole Bible can and should be brought to bear on the parenting process.

The Bible tells us who we are, how we got here, how sin devastated everything, how man is made right with God, and how to live our lives before a holy God.

So if parenting is basically discipling the people that God has placed in closest proximity to you, then the whole Bible can address the parenting task. A parent's primary job is to teach, reprove, correct, and train so nearly every passage applies. For instance, James 4:1–3 seems to indicate that one of the reasons we quarrel with one another is because we want something that we do not have. Do your children quarrel? Yes, and they do so because there is something they want that they are not getting. When they are little, it can be something as basic as a toy. As they grow older, it can be that they want (and are not receiving) something more sophisticated, like respect, appreciation, justice, or even love and affection. Does James say, "Parents, here's how you handle quarrelling children"? No. But this is a parenting verse that beats all parenting verses. Far from being anemic when it comes to parenting, the Bible speaks to any situation that a parent might encounter when discipling their children and trying to shape their hearts toward the gospel. It is a parent's responsibility, then, to make sure that they understand the Bible well enough to not only apply it to their own lives, but also to the lives of others, particularly their children. You cannot merely come up with your own strategy. You cannot choose to have no strategy at all. Biblically rooted parenting is not optional. The health of the home and church depend upon it.

The Priority of the Marriage

The second idea that evangelicals affirm when it comes to parenting is the priority of the marriage in the home. Adam and Eve were a family before kids came along. In Ephesians 5, the gospel picture of Christ and the church is depicted by the husband and wife. Children are an addition to the already existing family. Hopefully they are a welcomed addition, but an addition nevertheless. It is very common in the evangelical community for the home to increasingly become child-centered. After all, it is argued, don't we want them to have every confidence that they are the most significant priority to their parents so that they will have a high level of self-confidence? In order to get to this goal, parents will, with good intentions, so devote themselves to their children that they inadvertently create a disobedient and disruptive child. In an effort to demonstrate to the child that they are the most important thing to their parents, the child begins to believe what the parents are trying to communicate; namely, that they are more important than anything else.

Human beings were not designed by God to be the center of attention or to develop a sense of self-importance. The Bible regularly warns us to not think more highly of ourselves than we ought, and encourages us to see others as more important than ourselves. When a child begins to see themselves as the most important person in the home, he develops an attitude of entitlement that expects prioritization and even special treatment. This, in turn, cultivates pride in the life of the child. All of these attitudes and behaviors are listed as sinful in the Bible, and pride even invites the active opposition of God into one's life. So far from helping to raise an obedient, gospel-oriented child, this approach actually helps to train up a very disobedient one.

The strength of the home is rooted in the strength of the marriage. The strength of the relationship between parents and their children is rooted in the strength of the marriage. The stability of the child is rooted in the strength of the marriage. How does a younger child have a sense as to whether or not things are stable in the world? Are they reading the *Wall Street Journal*? Are they watching the evening news? Are they following the stock market? Of course not.

A child decides if things are stable in the world by their confidence in their parents' marriage. Now they are not sophisticated enough to explain such things about their own soul, but a rocky marriage displayed in front of a child will actually disrupt the child's very soul.

Over the years our various children have many times displayed uncharacteristically disobedient behavior. When this happens, we almost always will ask ourselves these questions: "Has this child observed us interacting in positive and even fun ways in the last several days? Have they seen us kiss or hug? Have they seen us enjoying one another's company? Laughing together?" If not, we immediately make every effort to remedy the situation. Parents who prioritize their children over their marriage are usually flabbergasted at how it impacts their children in the exact opposite way that they expected. Even older children draw comfort and confidence as they observe their parents show affection and kindness toward one another. So, far from feeling neglected, children in marriage-centered homes have the confidence that parents are actually looking for that cannot be found in making a child feel like they are the center of the universe.

The marriage can be prioritized in several ways. First, a husband and wife must carve out time daily to talk and debrief from the day. This is one of the best ways to communicate to one another and the children that the marriage relationship is most important. Often, we will intentionally have a conversation in the evenings and make the children go to their rooms. This does not make the children feel unwanted; it actually makes them feel secure even though they certainly would not be able to explain why. Second, a husband and wife should make the time to get away on a date three to four times per month. This does not have to be expensive, but it does need to be exclusive. No kids allowed. Third, it has served us well to get away for several days without the children two or three times per year. Again, this does not need to be expensive; it simply serves as another opportunity to enjoy the marriage, and send a clear message to one another and the children. Prioritizing the marriage not only brings security to children, but it also sets the marriage up as the primary example as parents authentically live out the gospel day in and day out in the home.

The Responsibility of Leadership

The third idea affirmed by evangelicals with regard to parenting is the responsibility of leadership. In Deuteronomy 6, God gives clear instruction to parents with regard to how they should instruct their children with His commands: "Repeat them to your children. Talk about them when you sit in your house and when you walk along the road, when you lie down and when you get up. Bind them as a sign on your hand and let them be a symbol on your forehead. Write them on the doorposts of your house and on your city gates" (Deut. 6:7–9). In other words, parents have an enormous responsibility to clearly and regularly through the normal ebb and flow of the day communicate the statutes and commands of God to their children. But with this responsibility comes authority. Paul clearly admonishes children to obey their parents in Ephesians 6. Parents, you are in authority over your children.

Authority is not valued in today's culture. From childhood we rarely want to be told what to do. In fact, in many circles bucking authority is valued. However, God has put authority structures everywhere.

In Genesis one can see immediately God's authority over the cosmos. Adam and Eve are given authority over the creation to subdue and exercise dominion over it. Adam demonstrates his authority over the animals by naming each of them. In the Old Testament, there are clear structures of authority as the people of God are led by prophets, priests, and kings. In the New Testament, wives are to be submissive to their husbands. All of us are to be submissive to government. Then, the books of Hebrews and 1 and 2 Timothy outline the structures for pastoral authority. And in Ephesians 6, Paul speaks directly to children, telling them they must obey their parents.

One of the reasons that authority is not fully appreciated in our culture is that many people have seen so many bad examples. It is important to be reminded, however, that authority is not for the good of the person by whom it is possessed. Authority is for the good of the people being led. In Deuteronomy 17, Moses puts forth some requirements for the king. One of his first acts is to produce his own handwritten copy of the law so that it will be in close proximity to him and he should "read from it all the days of his life" (Deut. 17:19). In other words, leadership begins with a proper understanding of the Word of God. It begins with a life devoted to its study. Just like kings, a parent's leadership should be an expression of godliness that comes from a careful intent to understand and obey the Bible. Moses also admonishes kings that they are not to acquire too many horses, too much gold, too much silver, or many wives for themselves. In other words, a king should not use this privileged office for his own gain or for his own self-aggrandizement. Parents, too, should note that their authority is given to the family by God and they are to assert this authority for the good of their children and not themselves.

For Christian parents, the balance between extreme expressions of authority and permission can be a challenge. Christians know that along with the high standards presented in Scripture, there are also themes of mercy, grace, and forgiveness. Sometimes parents are so permissive and are held hostage in their own homes because they are afraid of alienating their children. Sometimes parents are so demanding they cause resentment in their children. The solution to this tension is always predicated on the prioritization of the parents' personal walk with the Lord. Parents that are authentically pursuing Christ and His gospel will more likely be able to balance the relationship between authority and permissiveness.

Authority should always be balanced with love, affection, and frankly, fun. Over the years, we have discovered that high expectations with low levels of fun creates an oppressive environment. High levels of fun with low expectations create a foolish and immature environment.

The Secrecy of the Heart

The fourth parenting priority that evangelicals affirm is the secrecy of the heart. Proverbs 4:23 instructs us to "guard [our] heart above all else, for it is the source of life." As a parent, it is easy to become more preoccupied with external behavior than trying to deal with matters of the heart. The tiresome task of trying to understand motive can leave us satisfied with only a semblance of obedience that reflects outward conformity without the accompanying internal heart compliance. God, however, is more concerned about the heart. And behavior in our children reveals what is in the heart. In fact, it is the heart that actually determines behavior as Jesus said, "For from within, out of people's hearts, come evil thoughts, sexual immoralities, thefts, murders, adulteries, greed, evil actions, deceit, self-indulgence, envy, slander, pride, and foolishness. All these evil things come from within and defile a person" (Mark 7:21–23). How many of you are dealing with the same thing over and over with your children? The heart hasn't yet been reached. The heart has not changed. Many Christian parents are inadvertently raising Pharisees. Jesus had a vivid description for the Pharisees. He referred to them as whitewashed tombs. In other words, they were all cleaned up on the outside, but on the inside they were rotting flesh. On the inside they still stunk like a grave.

Part of reaching the child's heart is helping them with understanding their own motives. How many of you have asked your child when they've done something wrong, "Why did you do that?" We have all done it. What do they say? "I don't know." Do you know why they say that? They don't know! In fact, what would you want a four-year-old to say? "You see, there was this guy named Adam, and he had a wife named Eve. They ate some fruit they shouldn't have eaten, sin entered into the world. I've inherited the sin nature of Adam, now according to Romans 7, I do what I don't want to do, I don't do what I want to do . . ." You have to help them understand why they do what they do. You have to help them with the categories of idolatry, pride, covetousness, rejection of authority, dishonoring parents. What does this look like?

Years ago, our older two boys were about eight and six years old. Gunnar came running into the house with Fisher in tow, yelling, "Fisher almost got hit by a car! Fisher almost got hit by a car!" As Gunnar was recounting the near accident, Fisher apparently gave Gunnar a negative look. "Don't you give me that look," said Gunnar. "You've told on me several times this week and I've given you grace upon grace. No more! It's your turn!"

Well, at this point there is an obvious problem that eclipses Fisher's carelessness. Of course, we don't want Fisher to get hit by a car, but Gunnar had a real heart problem. You see, Gunnar came into the house as if his motivation was concern for his brother's well-being. He acted as if he really cared that his parents not experience the grief and heartache associated with a child being hit by a car. His real reason for telling on Fisher was revenge.

We have a couple of gaming systems in our home and we keep track of how often our children play them by using a pass system. Each younger child gets three thirty-minute passes each week; simple small squares of copy paper with their initials on it. When one of my middle daughters was about ten, I went to her room to see what she was up to. What I found was my sweet little girl sitting on her bed with copy paper and a pair of scissors, cutting out little squares about the size of a game pass. I said, "Payton, what are you doing?" Without missing a beat and with a sweet and innocent look on her face, she replied, "Just cutting paper, Daddy." That young lady had an entire counterfeit operation going on in that room. As you can see, she was not merely cutting paper. In her heart, she planned to deceive us by sneaking in a few extra opportunities to play one of the systems.

In both of these scenarios, the kids were all cleaned up on the outside, but on the inside they were like rotting flesh. This is why reaching the heart of your child is often described as one of the most difficult parts of parenting. Because there are so many daily needs to address the heart of the child, it is time consuming and takes enormous emotional energy. It can easily be neglected. The Christian parent then will take a long view and "not get tired of doing good, for we will reap at the proper time if we don't give up" (Gal. 6:9).

The Necessity of Discipline

The fifth parental affirmation for evangelicals is the necessity of discipline. Children do not come to us morally neutral. They have all inherited the sin nature of Adam and it doesn't take long before it is readily evident in their behavior. This requires the disciplinary involvement of the parents. This is at the heart of the need for discipline, but there are other key factors as well.

First, we discipline because we are in authority, which has already been addressed in this chapter. Second, we discipline because the Bible says that children are to obey. Paul told the children at Ephesus, "Children, obey your parents in the Lord, because this is right. Honor your father and mother, which is the first commandment with a promise, so that it may go well with you and that you may have a long life in the land" (Eph. 6:1–3). He also told the children in Colossae, "Children, obey your parents in everything, for this pleases the Lord" (Col. 3:20). Solomon admonishes his own son to "keep your father's command, and don't reject your mother's teaching" (Prov. 6:20).

While this is not exhaustive, the Bible is clear that children are to obey their parents.

Third, we discipline because children do not obey on their own. They have inherited the sin nature of Adam and are sinners by nature and by choice. Because of their sin, the Bible says, "foolishness is bound to the heart of a youth" (Prov. 22:15). It is the process of discipline that drives the foolishness from him. Fourth, we discipline to give our child their proper identity. Hebrews 12:7–8 explains, "Endure suffering as discipline: God is dealing with you as sons. For what son is there that a father does not discipline? But if you are without discipline—which all receive—then you are illegitimate children and not sons." One of the evidences that one is in Christ, is that God disciplines him. Children partially will find their identity in the home as children through the means of loving discipline. Fifth, we discipline because it yields right behavior. Hebrews 12:11 reminds us, "No discipline seems enjoyable at the time, but painful. Later on, however, it yields the peaceful fruit of righteousness to those who have been trained by it." Discipline yields right behavior, and the by-product of right behavior is peace.

Any form of discipline should be carried out by the parent with great humility. The Christian parent that is growing in Christ will regularly be reminded that they have no righteousness of their own. They are covered in the righteousness of Christ. As they are dealing with the sins of their children, they should be mindful of their own sin and their own dependence upon the gospel. This is the place at which parents often miss the opportunity to point their children to Christ. Often parents will correct and discipline with a heart of anger that will eventually push the child to embrace a works-centered righteousness and will even create a self-righteous heart in the parent. Paul, on the other hand, instructed the Galatians, "Brothers and sisters, if someone is overtaken in any wrongdoing, you who are spiritual, restore such a person with a gentle spirit, watching out for yourselves so that you also won't be tempted" (Gal. 6:1). Gentleness should be at the heart of any act of discipline, and this gentleness is an expression of humility because the believer knows that he himself has been forgiven much. Paul's warning about temptation stems from the fact that a lack of gentleness and humility in the disciplinary process leads to self-righteousness and a level of pride that makes the parent more vulnerable to sin in their own life.

The Reality of the Battle

The sixth key area of parental affirmation is the reality of the battle. The Bible is clear that we are in a battle and it all starts in the book of Genesis as God curses the serpent. God says, "I will put hostility between you and the woman, and between your offspring and her offspring. He will strike your head, and you will strike his heel" (Gen. 3:15). Not only is this the first offer of the gospel, it is also a declaration of war. The one who will crush and defeat Satan will be the offspring of the woman. No wonder Satan hates marriage and family. No wonder there is such a bull's-eye on the back of every home.

When my oldest son was about nine years old, we were riding in the car and he asked me if I had seen a particular movie. My answer was in the affirmative, so his natural next question was, "Was it any good?" Well, I thought the movie was terrible so I said, "It was the dumbest movie ever made by human hands. I want all of my brain cells back from when I watched it." The next question he asked bothered me, not because my kids are not allowed to ask questions, but because up to this point in his life, he had not questioned my judgment very much at all.

"When can I watch it?" he asked. I wondered where this seemingly sudden doubt came from, so I asked, "Are there times when you think there are really good things available to you that I know about, things that you would enjoy and would bless you, but I just withhold them from you?" His answer broke my heart. "Yes."

Do you see the perversion in this? Satan is tempting a nine-year-old boy to believe that his father, who claims to love him and care for him, does not really want good things for him. This is at the heart of a demonic strategy. Malachi seems to indicate that one of the evidences of the manifest presence of God is that hearts of fathers will be turned toward their sons and the hearts of sons will be turned toward their fathers, and by way of application, that hearts of parents will be turned toward their children and the hearts of children will be turned toward their parents. Right in the front seat of that car, the battle was raging.

This is why Paul tells the Ephesians, "Finally, be strengthened by the Lord and by his vast strength. Put on the full armor of God so that you can stand against the schemes of the devil. For our struggle is not against flesh and blood, but against the rulers, against the authorities, against the cosmic powers of this darkness, against evil, spiritual forces in the heavens" (Eph. 6:10–12). It often does not seem like we are in a battle. The comfort in which we live can create an illusion that things are really better than they are and this can lull us into a state of complacency and casualness. And then, many times when we do acknowledge the battle, we mistake its combatants as those who are flesh and blood. In the parenting task we often believe that the kids are our enemy when, in reality, it is the "spiritual forces of evil in the heavenly places."

While not exhaustive, this chapter has sought to highlight some key affirmations held by evangelicals with regard to parenting. May God be pleased through the Lord Jesus to strengthen marriages, help parents exercise Christlike authority over their children, and turn the hearts of children toward their parents and the hearts of parents toward their children so that the gospel will be effectively passed down from generation to generation.

Discussion Questions

· · · · · · · · · · · · · · · ·

1. What are examples of unbiblical parenting philosophies practiced by many in our culture (approaches to discipline, authority, etc.)? What convictions should Christian parents affirm to ensure their parenting is rooted in the gospel of Jesus Christ?

2. Why is it a mistake to think the Bible has little to say about parenting? How can the whole Bible be brought to bear on the task of parenting?

3. In what ways does a healthy marriage stabilize the home? Why is it destructive to prioritize children over marriage? What are some practical ways to prioritize marriage?

4. How can parents cultivate respect for authority in their home? What does the Bible teach about the ultimate purpose of parental authority?

5. What might persistent behavior problems indicate about the condition of a child's heart? In terms of discipline, why is addressing matters of the heart more important than external behavior modification?

CHAPTER

2

What Does the Gospel Say?

Timothy Paul Jones

"DADDY, YOU DIDN'T SAY ANYTHING ABOUT TWISTING PEOPLE'S arms," she said, and I discovered how dangerous a list of rules can be.[1]

The year that we adopted our oldest daughter, she attended first grade at a nearby Montessori school. There, she had some struggles when it came to interacting constructively with other children. To be specific, when things didn't go her way in a playgroup, someone inevitably ended up hurt, and that "someone" was never her.

Seeking to avoid a lawsuit, I made a list of practices that civilized people generally perceive as unacceptable ways to respond to one another. This list included the many activities that my daughter had already tried—hitting, kicking, punching, scratching—plus a few that she hadn't yet considered but probably soon would, such as detonating thermonuclear weaponry on the playground. Each morning, I went through the list with her and pointed out how God calls us to value every person as someone created in His image. Things went quite smoothly for almost a week. Then, on Friday afternoon, I received a call from the school.

"Your daughter has something that she would like to discuss with you," the school administrator said. She handed the telephone to my child, and the first words that I heard were, "Daddy, you didn't say anything about twisting people's arms." And she was right. I hadn't included that action on my list, and I was confronted with the danger of making a list of rules. Once we make a list, it's easy to assume that everything we should or shouldn't do is included in the list. As long as we stick to the list, everything is fine—or so we think.

Why Rules Are Necessary but Never Enough

The assumption that keeping a list of rules can make everything right isn't limited to arm-twisting seven-year-olds. "Human nature after the fall," a German preacher named Martin Luther once pointed out, "is no longer able to imagine or conceive any way to be made right with God other than works of the law."[2] Apart from the grace of God in Christ, every one of us tends to lapse into judging ourselves and others according to lists of rules.

The problem is that no list of rules can ever lead us or our children to life.

This isn't because rules are bad; it's because *we* are bad (Rom. 7:12; 1 Tim. 1:8). Lists of rules and laws can be helpful guides that reveal our shortcomings and restrain evil, but they can never produce the righteousness that leads to life (Rom. 4:13; Gal. 3:24). Only the gospel can fill our lives with true righteousness (Rom. 1:16; Gal. 3:6–9), and God gives us this righteousness through faith in the sacrifice of Jesus Christ. True life and righteousness come to us completely apart from any effort to check certain boxes or satisfy a list (Rom. 3:21; 10:4–13). "The law," evangelist D. L. Moody once pointed out, "can pursue a man to Calvary, but no further."[3]

As followers of Jesus Christ, we understand the centrality of the gospel and the limits of the law. And yet, when it comes to parenting, it can be difficult to see how the gospel should shape our day-by-day practices of guiding our children. Indeed, parenting seemingly requires an endless list of rules simply to increase the likelihood that our children survive childhood! If none of us made any rules for our children, our preschoolers would most likely spend their days picking their noses with paper clips, sliding butter knives into electrical outlets, and seeing how long the family's hamster might survive in the microwave. Even when children and teenagers grow older, they need limits to keep them from pursuing foolish and destructive paths. The problem is, sometimes, these lists and limits can become the primary focus of our parenting—despite the fact that we're fully aware that no law can produce lasting joy in this life or fruit that endures beyond this life.

In this chapter, I want to challenge you to ask yourself one simple question:

> *What might look different in my day-by-day practices of parenting if the gospel reshaped my perspectives and priorities?*

Before we begin to unpack some possible answers, I must admit to you that I am not speaking as a master who has reached a final destination; I'm writing as a pilgrim who is on a journey with you.

As the father of children who range in age from second grade to the second year of college, I am still struggling day-by-day to allow the gospel to reshape my practices of parenting. Gospel-shaped parenting is difficult, and I am reminded of that daily. It nails our pride-packed human agendas to a bloody cross and calls us to a purpose far greater than our plans or our children's happiness and success. Perhaps most difficult of all, it requires us to see our children as far more than our children and to release their futures to a God who loves them far more than we ever could.

With that in mind, let's look together at four ways that the gospel can reshape our parenting.

The Gospel Reshapes Parenting by Revealing a Child's True Identity

To see how the gospel reshapes parenting, let's first remind ourselves what the gospel *is* and what the gospel *does*.

The gospel is the good news that God has inaugurated His reign on earth through the life, death, and resurrection of the Lord Jesus Christ. When we repent and rely on Christ's righteousness instead of our own, His Kingdom power transforms us, and we become participants in the community of the redeemed. United with Christ through His Spirit, we are adopted as God's heirs, and we gain a new identity that transcends every earthly status. Husbands and wives, parents and children, orphans and widows, immigrants and citizens, the addict struggling in recovery and the teetotaling grandmother—all of us who are in Christ through the gospel become brothers and sisters, "heirs of God and coheirs with Christ" (Rom. 8:17; see also Matt. 12:50; Luke 20:34–48; Gal. 3:28–29; 4:3–7; Eph. 1:5; 2:13–22; Heb. 2:11; James 2:5; 1 Pet. 3:7).

So what does this mean for us as Christian parents?

It means that our children are far more than our children. Our children are, first and foremost, our potential or actual brothers and sisters in Christ.

Viewed in this way, our relationship with our children suddenly takes on a very different meaning. I will remain the father of my daughters until death, but—inasmuch as they embrace the gospel—I will remain their brother for all eternity.

As a parent, it is my responsibility to provide for my daughters and to prepare them for life; as their brother in the gospel, I am called to lay down my life for their sakes (1 John 3:16).

As a parent, I help them to see their own sin; as their brother, I am willing to confess my own sin (James 5:16).

As a parent, I speak truth into their lives; as a brother, I speak the truth patiently, ever seeking the peace that only the gospel can bring (Matt. 5:22–25; 1 Cor. 1:10; James 4:11; 5:7–9).

As a parent, I discipline my daughters so that they consider the consequences of poor choices; as a brother, I disciple, instruct, and encourage them to chase what is pure and good (Rom. 15:14; 1 Tim. 5:1–2).

As a parent, I help these children to recognize the right path; as their brother in the gospel, I pray for them and seek to restore them when they veer onto the wrong path (Matt. 18:21–22; Gal. 6:1; James 5:19–20; 1 John 5:16).

Your children and mine are also eternal beings whose days will long outlast the rise and fall of the kingdoms of the earth. They and their children and their children's children will flit ever so briefly across the face of this earth before being swept away into eternity (James 4:14). If our children become our brothers and sisters in Christ, their days upon this earth are preparatory for glory that will never end (Dan. 12:3; 2 Cor. 4:17–5:4; 2 Pet. 1:10–11). Children are wonderful gifts from God—but they are far more than gifts. Seen from the perspective of the gospel, every child in your household is, first and foremost, a potential or actual brother or sister in Christ. Whatever children stand beside us in eternal glory will not stand beside us as our children. They will stand beside us because—and only because—they have become our brothers and sisters in Christ.

Does this mean the parent-child relationship somehow passes away once a child becomes a brother or sister in Christ through the gospel? Of course not! The gospel doesn't cancel roles that are rooted in God's creation. Jesus and Paul freely appealed to the order of God's creation as a guide for leadership in the Christian community (Matt. 19:4–6; Mark 10:5–9; Acts 17:24–26; 1 Cor. 11:8–9; 1 Tim. 2:13–15). Far from negating the order of God's creation, the gospel adds a deeper and richer dimension that fulfills God's original design.

The Gospel Reshapes Parenting by Calling Parents to Become Disciple-Makers

So what happens when parents begin to see their children as potential or actual brothers and sisters in Christ? The writings of Paul provide us with a hint. The same apostle who called Timothy to encourage younger believers as Christian brothers and sisters also commanded fathers to nurture their offspring "in the training and instruction of the Lord" (Eph. 6:4; see also Col. 3:21). In other letters, Paul applied these same two terms—*discipline* and *instruction*—to patterns that characterize disciple-making relationships among brothers and sisters in Christ. For Paul, *discipline* is the result of being trained in the words of God (2 Tim. 3:16), and *instruction* refers to admonitions and guidance to avoid unwise behaviors and ungodly teachings (1 Cor. 10:11; Titus 3:9–10).

Seen in this light, Paul's command to nourish children in the "discipline and instruction" of Christ suggests that Paul was calling parents—and particularly fathers—to do more than simply manage their children's behaviors and provide for their needs. As believers in Jesus Christ, we are called to relate to our children just as we would respond to nonbelievers in the world or young believers in our church. We are responsible for speaking the gospel to them and we are called to train them in the ways of Christ (Matt. 28:19–20). God's creation and humanity's fall have positioned parents as providers and disciplinarians. Through the gospel, Christian parents have been called to become disciple-makers as well.

This process of parental disciple-making will certainly look different for every family. In my household, it means a family devotional every Sunday evening, intertwined with daily prayers and weekly discipleship times with each of my children. In another household, it might look like nightly family devotions combined with spiritual debriefings after movies and sporting events. Likewise, for other families it may take the form of songs and Scriptures memorized in the car during morning commutes.

The approach you take toward discipling your children is negotiable; the practice itself is not.

This is not to suggest that Christian parents should become their children's sole instructors in Scripture! After all, the Great Commission to make disciples was given to the whole church as a calling to reach the whole world, including children (Matt. 28:19). While discipleship and spiritual formation concern the church as a whole, it is the duty of Christian parents to prioritize and implement consistent practices of discipleship with their own children.

The Gospel Reshapes Parenting by Providing Us with a Purpose Larger Than This Life

A few years ago, a survey asked parents how they would know if they had been successful in their parenting. The most popular answers were that successful parenting means raising children who are happy and have good values. The response ranking third centered on the child's success in his or her vocation.[4] If this survey rightly represents parents' real priorities, fathers and mothers are focused on raising children who act good, feel good, and attain financial success.

Morality, happiness, and success aren't bad, of course—but they are miserable goals for parenting. If these goals are our definition of successful parenting, the gospel is not shaping our day-by-day parental practices. Apart from the gospel of Jesus Christ, focusing on good morals tends to result either in self-righteousness or rebellion in our children. What makes our children happy in the short term may not direct them toward Jesus Christ in the long term, and financial success is no guarantee of lasting joy or peace. None of these values last past this life. And yet, these are the dominant values in our culture when it comes to parenting.

Now, if children were nothing more than a gift for this life, a single-minded focus on their happiness and success might actually make sense. As long as the family's chaotic schedule secures a spot for the child in a top-tier university, forfeiting intentional spiritual formation for the sake of competitive sports leagues and advanced-placement classes would be understandable—if children were a gift for this life only. Working round-the-clock would be permissible, provided that your children's friends are visibly impressed with the house you can barely afford. If children were a gift for this life only, it might make sense to raise children with calendars that are full but souls that are empty, making them captives of the deadly delusion that their value depends on what they accomplish here and now.

But the gospel calls us to seek a purpose for our children that is so much larger than this life.

Even before humanity's fall into sin, God designed the raising of children to serve as a means for the multiplication of His manifest glory around the globe (Gen. 1:26–28). A few bites of forbidden fruit, raising Cain as well as Abel, and a worship service that ended in fratricide took their toll on that first family—but God refused to give up on His first purpose to turn the family into a means for the revelation of His glory. God promised that, through the offspring of Eve, He would send a Redeemer to crush the satanic serpent's skull and to flood the earth with glory divine (Gen. 3:15; 4:1, 25; Hab. 2:14). From the beginning to the end of God's plan, the family has been His chosen pathway for the defeat of darkness, the revelation of His glory, and the passing of His story from one generation to the next.

What this means practically is that we should view our children in light of a larger purpose. We should see them as potential bearers of the gospel to generations yet unborn. In God's good design, our children will most likely raise children who will in turn beget more children. How we mold our children's souls while they reside in our households will shape the lives of children who have yet to draw their first gasp of air (Ps. 78:6–7). That's why our primary purpose for our children must not be anything so small and miserable as temporary success.

"For what does it benefit someone to gain the whole world and yet lose his life?" Jesus asked His first followers (Mark 8:36). When it comes to our children, we might ask a similar question:

- What does it profit your child to gain an academic scholarship and yet never experience consistent prayer and devotional times with his parents?
- What will it profit my child to succeed in a sport and yet never know the rhythms of a home centered on Christ, where we are willing to release any dream at any moment if we become too busy to disciple one another?
- What will it profit the children all around us in our churches if they are accepted into the finest colleges and yet never leverage their lives for the sake of proclaiming the gospel to the nations?

In the beginning, God infused humanity with a yearning for eternity (Eccl. 3:11). If the scope of our vision for our lives or for the lives of our children shrinks any smaller than eternity, our thirst for eternity will drive us to fill the emptiness with a multitude of lesser goals and lower gods—including the fleeting happiness and success of our children. When the happiness and success of children becomes the controlling framework for life, parents expect their children to have, to do, and to be more than anyone else, and they are willing to sacrifice family discipleship and the proclamation of the gospel to achieve this objective.

I am not suggesting that success in academics or athletics or vocation somehow stand outside God's good plan. Learning and play are joys that God Himself wove into the very fabric of creation. Although cursed in the Fall, work was also a part of God's good design before the Fall (Gen. 2:15; 3:17–23). And yet, whenever any activity—no matter how good it may be—becomes amplified to the point that no margin remains for family members to disciple one another or to share the gospel in the world around us, a joy has been distorted into an idol. Our purpose in everything that we do as parents should be to leverage our children's lives to advance God's Kingdom so that people in every tribe and every nation gain the opportunity to respond in faith to the rightful King of kings.

There are a couple of phrases that I have repeated over and over throughout my children's lives, particularly when they're considering vocational possibilities. What I've said to them is simply this: "I would rather have you on the other side of the world seeking God's glory than in a house next door to me seeking your glory, and I would rather have you in a grave in God's will than in a mansion resisting God's will." A few weeks ago, one of my children put these statements to the test.

Our oldest daughter had chosen counseling as her major before starting college, and she was halfway through her first semester of the degree. One afternoon, she met me at a coffee shop, and we began to talk about how she might use her education in the future.

"Dad," she said after a few minutes. "Did you know I'm not in the degree program I'm supposed to be?"

"No," I said, with a bit of confusion. "What degree should you be in?"

"I'm supposed to be in missions, but I don't know if I want to be that far from my family."

This admission opened a door in our conversation, and we stepped through it ever so gingerly, exploring a calling that my daughter had sensed for some time. There were a few tears and a lot of questions, but in the end she settled on switching her degree program from counseling to global studies.

As we got up from the table, she said to me, "You always said you'd rather me be on the other side of the world in God's will than to be right next to you outside God's will, but I never knew if that was for real or not."

The only honest answer I could give her was this: "Neither did I. But I hoped it was; I always hoped."

God calls us—just as He called our father Abraham—to be willing to release every longing for our children's safety and success for the sake of obedience to God's Word (Gen. 22:2–18).

Not every child will—or should—grow up to be a missionary on the other side of the world. But every child is called to place God's Kingdom first wherever they are, and every Christian parent is called to be willing to seek the spread of God's Kingdom above and beyond every earthly comfort or success.

This attitude does not come to us easily. In fact, this willingness doesn't come from us at all! Nothing less than the work of God through His Holy Spirit can create this willingness within us. And yet, what God asks of us in releasing our children to join His mission is no less than what He Himself has already done in Jesus Christ: "He did not even spare his own Son but offered him up for us all" (Rom. 8:32).

The Gospel Reshapes Parenting by Freeing Us from the Belief that Our Value Depends on Our Parenting

The longer I've been a parent, the more I've found myself taking refuge in one final truth about the gospel and parenting. The truth that has become my refuge is this:

Because of the grace that comes through the gospel, God's disposition toward me does not depend on how I perform as a parent. I did nothing to gain God's favor, and there's nothing I can do to keep God's favor. Through faith, I have been adopted in Christ (Rom. 8:15–17; Gal. 3:26). Because I am in Christ,

God the Father can never think anything less of me than He thinks of His beloved Son, Jesus Christ.

So what does this truth have to do with parenting?

Everything!

Meditate for a moment on the implications of this truth. Because of the gospel, God's approval of you doesn't depend on whether you provide your children with everything that everyone else thinks they need. God's approval of you doesn't depend on how your children act in the checkout line at the grocery store. It doesn't depend on whether your children grow up breast-fed, potty-trained by two years old, classically educated, and protected from artificial preservatives. It doesn't even depend on whether your children persist in the faith past the pomp and circumstance of their high school graduations. The good news of the gospel declares that God's approval of you doesn't depend on anything you do; it depends solely on what Christ has already done. All that any of us must do—which is really no "doing" at all—is to receive what God in Christ has already done.

The implications of this simple truth for parenting are staggering, and I desperately need to be reminded of them every day. Because we no longer have to prove ourselves through perfect performances, we can humble ourselves and ask for our family's forgiveness when we fail. When we feel overwhelmed as parents, we can cry out for help. When we say no to commitments that would consume our calendars and our souls, we can do so without the guilt and fear that grows out of our desperate yearning for the approval of others. We can be set free from our nagging desire to demonstrate our own righteousness by demanding that other parents measure up to our family's standards. We can guide our children toward Christ from a foundation of joy and rest, knowing that God has already delivered to us everything that He demands from us.

There is no list of rules for gospel-shaped parenting; there are no items to check off as you complete them. There is, however, Christ Himself. Jesus has given us His Word, His Spirit, His people, and His gospel. In all of our efforts as parents, our goal is not merely to arrive at the end of the day with the same number of children we had at the beginning of the day. Our goal is a Kingdom that never ends, and our purpose in parenting is to see this Kingdom revealed through our families.

Discussion Questions

1. When, in your parenting, are you most likely to become so focused on lists and rules that you lose sight of the gospel? What could you do, in light of this chapter, to maintain the centrality of the gospel in your practices of parenting?

2. Here's how the gospel has been defined in this chapter: "The gospel is the good news that God has inaugurated His reign on earth through the life, death, and

resurrection of the Lord Jesus Christ. When we repent and rely on Christ's righteousness instead of our own, His Kingdom power transforms us, and we become participants in the community of the redeemed." List three ways, in addition to the ones described in this chapter, that the gospel can reshape your day-by-day practices of parenting.

3. What do you do on a regular basis to disciple your children? Discuss with a group of Christian parents what you and they are doing to train and instruct the next generation. Learn everything that you can from other families' discipleship practices and encourage any parents who are struggling in this area.

4. Before reading this chapter, had you ever thought of your children as potential or actual brothers and sisters in Christ? In what specific ways could this truth transform the ways that you choose to respond to your children in the upcoming week? How might your family's schedule change if you began to think of your children first and foremost as potential or actual brothers and sisters in Christ?

3

How Should the Christian Live?

Tedd and Margy Tripp

MANY PEOPLE WHO WANT TO HAVE CHILDREN FIND THAT they do not enjoy being parents. Parenting is not only hard work, it is heart work. It involves pouring out your life as you pour yourself into your children. Raising our children is one of the most important callings God has entrusted to us. The opportunity to provide a nurturing home in which our children are taught to love God and others is a high and holy calling.

Let's consider three elements of parenting that must be woven together in the nurturing process: communication that enables us to understand and engage our children; gospel-centered discipline, correction, and motivation; and finally, displaying God's glory for our children in the daily challenges of life.

Communication

Most of us think of communication as the ability to express our ideas. We think we have communicated when we have expressed our ideas and thoughts. In reality, the finest art of communication is the ability to understand the person with whom I am speaking.

The book of Proverbs speaks to this issue with great insight: "A fool does not delight in understanding, but only wants to show off his own opinions" (Prov. 18:2).

I had a conversation with my son near bedtime. I said what I thought needed to be said; he listened politely. "Well," I said, after finishing my speech, "I am glad we had this chance to talk." I prayed with him and went to bed. A few minutes later, there was a knock at our bedroom door.

"Dad, are you guys still awake?"

"Yeah, come on in. What's up?"

"Well, Dad, I just wanted to say that when you left my room you said, 'I'm glad we had this chance to talk,' and I just wanted to say that I didn't say anything."

"Oh, I see. I had a good talk; you had a good listen, right?"

"Yeah, sort of."

"Forgive me. If I had given you a chance to talk, what would you have said?"

"Oh, I don't know," he replied, "I just wanted to say that I didn't say anything."

What's the subtext here? "If you really want to know, you're going to have to work harder than that, Dad. I am not going to be that easy."

I was a fool that night. I could have said everything I had to say in the context of asking good questions. I could have expressed love and regard for him by striving to understand him and see things through his eyes. I could have made him feel known and understood. But I was a fool. My only thought was what I had to say. I did not take the time to draw him out. If I had delighted in understanding, I could have spoken with greater clarity and insight. If I had delighted in understanding, he could have left the conversation feeling that he was more important than just what I had to say. Proverbs 18:13 is similar: "The one who gives an answer before he listens—this is foolishness and disgrace for him." How many times have I answered before listening? I could anticipate what my child had to say; I lacked the patience to allow him to say it. I answered without really listening.

"I know what you are going to ask. The answer is, 'No!'"

"But, Dad."

"What part of, 'No!' don't you understand?"

"But, Dad, I didn't even ask my question."

"You don't have to ask your question. I'm your father. 'Before a word is on your tongue I know it altogether,' isn't that in the Bible somewhere?"

Your son or daughter never leaves that exchange feeling thankful for a mom or dad who is a mind reader! They feel they can't even gain a hearing. They wonder, why bother trying to communicate. They feel stifled and frustrated.

In Proverbs 20:5, there is a wonderful description of biblical communication, "Counsel in a person's heart is deep water, but a person of understanding draws it out." This is what we must do as we communicate with our children. They need a parent with understanding who can draw out the deep waters.

Ask good questions, questions that cannot be answered, "Yes" or "No." Train yourself to listen. Listen not only to what is being said, but also for what is not being said. Follow up answers with new questions. Let your child know that you delight in understanding them, not in simply airing your own opinion.

The incarnation of Jesus Christ illustrates this kind of communication. In the incarnation God entered into our world. He could have stayed off in heaven and shouted instructions to us. He could have spoken to us through a thick cloud, lightning, and thunder as He did in Exodus 19. Instead, He came to earth. He took on flesh like ours. He had a human psychology. Without ever sinning, He entered into all the experiences of life in a fallen world. He was tired and hungry at Jacob's well in John 4. He was thirsty. He asked the first person who came along for a drink. He wept at Lazarus's tomb. He fully entered our world. He can look at the world through our eyes.

According to Hebrews 2, His experience of life in this world gives Him the capacity to help us in our troubles: "For since he himself has suffered when he was tempted, he is able to help those who are tempted" (Heb. 2:18). The experience of living as a man, faced with temptation, enables Jesus to help us when we are tempted.

Jesus can look at the world through our eyes. He intimately knows our struggles and the struggles of our children. He became a man so that He could understand life in our world and help us in our times of temptation.

That's the note of triumph in Hebrews 4. "Therefore, since we have a great high priest who has passed through the heavens—Jesus the Son of God—let us hold fast to our confession. For we do not have a high priest who is unable to sympathize with our weaknesses, but one who has been tempted in every way as we are, yet without sin. Therefore, let us approach the throne of grace with boldness, so that we may receive mercy and find grace to help us in time of need" (Heb. 4:14–16). We acknowledge, to our shame, that sometimes our children have had a mom and dad who were unable to sympathize with their weaknesses.

What Jesus did for you and me is what we must do for our children. We must enter into their world and delight in understanding them. Have you ever had the experience of being with someone who was genuinely interested in knowing you? Do you remember what it is like to sense that your thoughts and ideas matter to someone? If you have ever had such an experience, you will remember that you delighted in that conversation.

If you want to be able to communicate with clarity, if you want to shepherd the hearts of your children, you must be able to see things as they see them. When you understand your children that thoroughly, you will be able to speak truth to them in ways that are both compelling and gracious.

Centrality of the Gospel

Keeping the gospel central in parenting our children is a daily challenge. There are many temptations to leave out the grace and the hope of the gospel when your children require correction and motivation.

How does keeping the gospel central look and sound? Your message to your children is this, "There is hope for people who fail, like you and Mom and Dad, and it is found in the God of grace." You could think of it this way: the gospel must be the core of your nurturing interaction with your children. The gospel is more than just the simple plan of salvation. It is all the grace and power of God addressed to our most profound needs—the need

for forgiveness, cleansing, internal transformation, and empowerment (Ezek. 36:25–26).

All Christian parents want their children to know, understand, and embrace the gospel of grace, but often we fail to direct
them to the gospel in their times of greatest need. This is the
essence of shepherding the heart. The temptation is to focus on
behavioral change. Whenever behavior becomes the goal, you are
prey to all the temptations to manipulate behavior.

> You might bribe—"If you are really good, I'll . . ."

> You might threaten—"You don't even want to know
> what will happen if you don't . . ."

> You might shame—"I can't believe that you children are
> so unkind and mean to each other . . ."

Each of these examples and many others are simply ways to
secure good behavior without addressing the heart or keeping the
power of the gospel before you and your children.

Whenever you are simply trying to secure proper behavior,
the power of the gospel and grace will never be the heart of your
nurture of your children. Behaviorism and the gospel don't mix.
They reflect two different and competing approaches to change.
Behaviorism seeks to produce change through appeal to the
child's crass self-interest. The gospel produces change that comes

through conviction of sin and faith in the power of Christ to forgive, renew, and empower your child to love God and others.

If the grace of the gospel and the need for internal change is not your message, if the heart is not addressed, only behavior, you will miss valuable opportunities to take your children to the cross for repentance, forgiveness, and cleansing.

- You will focus on externals and be less alert to pride, unbelief, idols of the heart, legalism, fear of man, pride in performance, compulsive self-love, and other intangible activities of the heart.
- You will not help your children understand hidden patterns of sin and unbelief—the secret, sneaky, self-deceptive ways of sin.
- You will tend to produce children who conform to the law outwardly while inwardly they are wracked by self-righteous pride and unbelief.
- You will miss the whole issue of motivation—good behavior can sometimes be produced by wrong motives.

Children need help understanding that behind every wayward act is a wayward heart. You want to help them become experts at diagnosing their heart disease.

The Bible bristles with information about the attitudes of the heart that lay beneath the things we say and do, both good and bad. Remember, it is out of the overflow of the heart that the mouth speaks (Luke 6:45). Sinful attitudes such as pride, self-love, hatred, envy, covetousness, fear of man, desire to be approved by others, rebellion, bitterness, vengeance, and many more lie behind the wrongful things children say and do. In the same way, kindness, love, gentleness, and humility are some of the gospel motivations for godly behavior.

Internal issues are the "why" of bad behavior. The external issues are the "what" or "when" of behavior. The need for grace is apparent when one thinks about internal issues. When confronted in kind ways during discipline and correction with the ugliness of pride or self-love, your children have no hope but the power of grace. Only the grace, forgiveness, cleansing, and empowerment of the gospel can enable your kids to know internal change. It is that internal change that is the ultimate goal of your nurturing care of your children.

Godly nurture and shepherding must target the heart! What you desire from your children is not just externally appropriate responses (I hear someone say, "I would be happy for even that"), but hearts that are changed. You long for them to see that their hearts have strayed from God's ways like lost sheep and that Christ came to produce change at the root that would also transform the fruit.

Keeping the gospel central does wonderful things for correction and discipline. It keeps you from hypocrisy and keeps you from missing the gospel of grace. You can identify with a child who is struggling with selfishness, because you understand how selfishness works in the human heart. You know what it is to be so mired in self-love that you will do anything to serve yourself and avoid serving others.

In those times when you can stand alongside this child, whose life is stained by self-love, the gospel is the basis for hope. Christ offers Himself to fallen humanity as the willing, able, powerful, Savior of sinners. There is hope for people whose lives are marked by compulsive self-love. Christ will forgive, cleanse, transform, and empower. You can share times when you have known freedom from selfishness and fear because of the power and grace of the gospel.

When you know your children are struggling, it is the gospel that will provide hope and help. We observed a wonderful conversation between one of our sons and his three-year-old son.

"It is hard to trust Daddy and obey, isn't it, son?"

"Yes." His son nodded.

"You know who helps Daddy obey?"

"Jesus?"

"That's right, Jesus helps me to obey and He can help you to obey. Let's pray to Jesus and ask Him to help you obey Daddy."

There is another wonderful benefit of keeping the gospel central. The gospel motivates obedience. In Titus 3, the apostle Paul recalls the grace of the gospel. He reminds his reader of what he and they were like, "foolish, disobedient, deceived, enslaved by various passions and pleasures" (Titus 3:3). He recalls also the invasion of grace in his life, speaking of the kindness and love of God who appeared with salvation, through washing and renewal and not because of righteousness in them. Then Paul says to Titus, I want you to stress the power and grace of the gospel, "so that those who have believed God might be careful to devote themselves to good works" (Titus 3:8).

Think about that! What motivates doing good? It is the gospel. The grace, mercy, and power of the gospel motivate Christians to devote themselves to doing what is good.

May God give you wisdom to keep the gospel central as you shepherd the hearts of your children.

Vision for God's Glory

Human beings are worshippers. It follows then, that children, too, are worshippers. I can almost hear someone say, "Not my children, Tedd and Margy, they fall asleep in church every week."

But it is true, your children worship. Your kids are made in the image of God. The world in which they live is designed to display the glory of God, and children—indeed, all human beings—are uniquely designed for worship. Like explorers driven to find distant shores, your sons and daughters go off every day in search of excitement. They are looking for something to answer the question, "Who or what is worth worshipping?"

The fact that human beings are hardwired for worship is unique in the creation. It is the reason we love to hear a symphony or watch a juggler or marvel at some feat of athleticism. We love to be dazzled. It is the reason we watch sports on TV. Do you know there are no diving competitions for penguins in the Antarctic? They perform marvelous dives without color commentary or slow-motion replays. A brown bear grabs a salmon from the Columbia River, by any account an amazing feat of timing and coordination, and yet no bears line the shore to applaud. Human beings do this sort of thing because human beings are uniquely designed for worship. Your kids love to be entranced by something amazing. They are instinctively worshippers.

What happens when children who are designed for worship fail to worship the God in whose image they have been made? Your kids do not cease to be worshippers; they simply worship and serve something else. The apostle speaks of this in Romans 1:25, "They exchanged the truth of God for a lie, and worshiped and served what has been created instead of the Creator, who is praised forever."

This is what your children do; it is what all humanity does. If your children do not worship and serve God, they do not cease to be worshippers, they simply make an exchange. They substitute something for God; they worship and serve something in the creation instead. They manufacture an idol—a substitute for God.

These idols your children find are not small statues; they are subtler than that. Leaving a Chinese restaurant with two young granddaughters, I felt a tug on my coat. "Grandpa," one asked, pointing to a large statue of Buddha in the corner, "Who's that fat man?" The question provided a wonderful opportunity to speak to the girls about idols. There are so many idols the human heart creates:

Pride and performance. Some children will lay all at the altar of performance. They are driven. The joys of performance and the praises that attend excellence are like a drug for them. Their joy is not in God's gifts to them, but in the intoxication of praise and attention.

Power and influence. Other children exhibit a lust to control the people in their world. These are the organizers and arrangers. If the game is playing school, they will always be the teachers. Their leadership skills are not the problem here, rather their desire for power over the people in their world controls them.

Pleasure and sensuality. You may have a thrill seeker in your family. This is the child who is always looking for the rush of some exciting, heart-throbbing, and adrenalin-pumping experience. They find the joys of ordinary living boring. Work seems to be a burden rather than fulfilling, because having fun has become a must to be okay.

Possessions. Some kids crave stuff. They pour through the catalogs that come to your home. They collect stuff; they polish stuff. When they leave the house they want to be assured that no one will touch their stuff while they are gone. Getting new stuff is the path to slaking whatever makes them unhappy or discontented at the moment.

We could add to the list of idols. People are endlessly creative when it comes to finding substitutes for God. For some children it may be fear of man, the desire for approval, friendship, or being someone, or having something that's "cool" is what life is about. It is useful to ask oneself, "What things are in my own life that are substitutes for God?" This pattern will help our children identify their own substitutes. It is sobering, but sanctifying.

The most important job you have as a parent is to show the glory of God to your children who are compulsively worshippers. Your kids are hardwired for worship, but in their fallen state, they instinctively worship and serve created things rather than God.

Psalm 145:1–4 talks about this when it says,

> I exalt you, my God the King, and bless your name
> forever and ever. I will bless you every day; I will
> praise your name forever and ever. The LORD is great
> and highly praised; his greatness is unsearchable. One
> generation will declare your works to the next and
> will proclaim your mighty acts.

Parents, you are the generation commending the glory and excellence of God to the next generation (see also Ps. 78:1–7).

Help your children see that the greatest joys are found in the nearness of God rather than in fulfilling their appetites.

> Many are asking, "Who can show us any good?" Let the light of your face shine on us, LORD. You have put more joy in my heart than they have when their grain and new wine abound. (Ps. 4:6–7)

Help your children see that the greatest joys are not the joys of having stuff or doing fun things, but the joys of knowing God.

Show your thrill seekers that the lasting joys and pleasures which people crave are found in knowing God.

> You reveal the path of life to me; in your presence is abundant joy; at your right hand are eternal pleasures. (Ps. 16:11)

Eternal pleasures, pleasures that will never go flat or stale, are found in the presence of God and nowhere else.

Illustrate for them that the greatest deliverance from adversity is not being delivered from difficulty (Ps. 27:1–3), but rather enjoying the beauty of the Lord.

> I have asked one thing from the LORD; it is what I desire: to dwell in the house of the LORD all the days of my life, gazing on the beauty of the LORD and seeking him in his temple. (Ps. 27:4)

Other psalms to which you may turn to underscore the joys and delights of being entranced by God would be Psalms 36:5–9; 63:1–5; 73:25–26; 81:10–16; and 96:1–6.

Why is this so important?

First, your kids do not live out of the facts and circumstances of their existence. They interpret everything that occurs in their lives. Their interpretation determines how they respond. The key to correctly interpreting life is the being and glories of the God for whom they are made. If they are worshiping and serving idols, they will never interpret the circumstances of life accurately.

Second, since you love your kids and desire their happiness, you will always be tempted to feed their idols. Many parents do just that. They fill their children's lives with stuff; they take delight in their children's delight in possessions. Yet they cling to the hope that someday their children will see that life is not found in possessions, but in knowing God. Resist the temptation to polish your kid's idols.

Obviously, if you are to show your children God's glories, you must be dazzled by Him yourself. Your delight in God is more persuasive than thousands of words.

The Christian life begins with glory. "For God who said, 'Let light shine out of darkness,' has shone in our hearts to give the light of the knowledge of God's glory in the face of Jesus Christ" (2 Cor. 4:6). The Christian life continues and grows as we behold God's glory. "We all, with unveiled faces, are looking [beholding or contemplating] as in a mirror at the glory of the Lord and are being transformed into the same image from glory to glory; this is from the Lord who is the Spirit" (2 Cor. 3:18).

Perhaps the best thing you could do for your children would be to get yourself before God, behold His glory, and then move toward your children with the encouragement that there is a great and glorious God for whom they were made. Life is found in beholding and knowing Him.

Each of us are different as parents and we bring differing insights to the task of raising children, but these three elements can enable us to shepherd them with wisdom. Delight in understanding your children. Strive to understand them. Keep the gospel central, so you are not just urging proper behavior, but pointing them to the willing, able, powerful Savior of sinners. Show them the transcendent glory and beauty of the God for whom they were made.

Discussion Questions

1. Why is listening an important part of parenting? How can cultivating this discipline help draw out the "deep waters" in our children?

2. What does Christ's incarnation and the gospel teach us about communication? What does this reveal about God, and how should this affect the way we interact with our children?

3. Why is it wrong to separate behavior change from the reality and power of the gospel? How does the gospel influence the task of discipline, and why is it important to address underlying heart issues?

4. What role does worship have in the task of parenting? How can parents direct the worship of their children to God?

How Should the Church Engage?

Candice and Steve Watters

THE MIDWEEK SERVICE OF THE CHURCH WE ATTENDED IN Colorado provided Scripture memorization exercises for young kids. That arrangement also provided us a perfect window of time for a midweek date. For a couple of weeks, we enjoyed coffee and adult conversation at the Starbucks nearby—until we found out that wasn't how the church intended the arrangement to work. We came to realize that they had not organized their Scripture memory program in order to meet our need for free babysitting and a date.

What can parents realistically expect from church? What parenting needs should a church prioritize?

Parents have no shortage of needs and concerns that the local church could address in some way: discipline, discipleship, media discernment, navigating a hostile culture, coping with the daily demands of raising young children, as well as guidance for a range of challenges such as sibling rivalry, sleep problems, eating issues, learning problems, bed-wetting, and more.

And there's no shortage of ways churches can go about engaging those needs and concerns. In fact, we're aware of churches currently providing the following programs, events, or resources as a ministry to parents: parenting conferences, father/daughter purity events, family camping trips, family mission trips, intergenerational events, family festivals, special celebrations of parenting milestones (such as baby dedications, passage to adolescence, baptism, graduation, etc.), preschool, parents' day out programs, meetings for moms of preschoolers, family resource libraries, parent-training series, home visitation programs, and distinctive ministries to single parents, blended families, parents of children with special needs, military families, grandparents (especially those providing primary care for their grandchildren because of absent parents), and people caring for children while also caring for aging parents.

To this list, you could also add numerous programs and events from Sunday school and Vacation Bible School to concerts, sports programs, and youth activities that have the secondary goal of serving parents in the process of serving their children. How much support and guidance should parents expect from a church, and how much effort and expense should churches take on in order to serve parents well?

We have been parents for sixteen years. We've experienced the flood of parenting programs, events, and resources from the large church we attended in Colorado. We have also witnessed the more modest offerings from churches under five hundred members. We gained a wealth of family and ministry advice while working at Focus on the Family for thirteen years, and we have continued to learn over the past six years through studying family discipleship while serving in a seminary community.

Our purpose in this chapter is to provide guidance for those seeking to serve parents in the local church. It certainly requires biblical wisdom to accomplish this task in a focused and fruitful way. We also want to encourage parents to *avail* themselves of what the local church is best positioned to provide them. We realize "avail" isn't an everyday verb, but this King-James-sounding word, meaning "to turn to your benefit," describes well how we as parents should actively embrace what is made available to us, by God's design, in the local church.

From our study of God's revelation in Scripture and our observations of parents and church leaders seeking to apply that biblical wisdom to our question, we have identified two primary commitments that the local church should embrace to best help parents flourish. The first commitment is to help fathers and mothers live out what is known as "the vocation of parenting" through the means of grace in the local church: the Word, prayer, and fellowship. The second commitment is for pastors, elders, and deacons to lead faithfully in their own homes as they serve pastorally in the church as loving, committed parents.

These commitments are simple and yet profoundly clarifying for setting parental expectations, in guiding the church's priorities in serving parents, and in shaping how the church's efforts are implemented.

The Vocation of Parenting and the Primary Means of Grace in the Local Church

First, what do we mean by helping men and women live out "the vocation of parenting" by serving them with "the means of grace" in the local church?

At a basic level, the local church should concentrate its energy on helping men and women understand and live out their parenting as *a calling to love and serve their children*—that's the basic definition of *vocation*. And we mean that the church should seek first and foremost to provide that help through preaching, fellowship, and prayer—which are the God-given vehicles for blessing His people in the body of Christ.

A church seeking to serve parents may offer a variety of programs, events, and resources while ultimately failing to produce lasting fruit if they lack a vision for the vocation of parenting. Parenting is not simply one of many areas of felt needs in a congregation. God created the family as the first institution and called men and women to love and serve in the vocations of husband and wife and father and mother.

The word we know as *vocation* is the Latinate version of the English word *calling*. All that's involved in parenting—feeding, clothing, bathing, disciplining, providing, housing, protecting, comforting, coaching—is not just a collection of tasks and duties, but is instead a calling that is spiritually significant for both God's purposes in the world and our individual lives. This is the doctrine of vocation that Martin Luther preached, drawn primarily from 1 Corinthians 7:17, where Paul writes, "Let each one live his life in the situation the Lord assigned when God called him." Luther taught that while God could have populated the earth by forming each new person from dust (as He did with Adam), instead God ordained that men and women should marry, have babies, and raise them together. As a result, the roles of husband, wife, and parents are vocations through which God works to raise and care for children.

"It is in our various vocations that we live out our faith in love and service to the various neighbors that God brings into our lives," writes Gene Edward Veith Jr., in his book *Family*

Vocation: God's Calling in Marriage, Parenting, and Childhood. "God doesn't need our good works," Luther proclaimed, "but our neighbor does."[5] In this, Luther implored men and women to see how God works not only *in* their lives, but *through* their lives—as a means of accomplishing His purposes. Veith explains this further:

> The good works we need to do as Christians—the arena of our sanctification—are not elaborate spiritual exercises or spectacular feats of accomplishment. Rather, they are to be found in our ordinary interactions with the actual human beings who God brings into our lives every day: the way we treat our spouse, the things we do for our children, what we do for our customers and fellow workers, how we get along with the other Christians in our church, how we treat the people we meet in the broader society. Our faith, "working through love" (Gal. 5:6), bears fruit in vocation. It is precisely in marriage, parenthood, economic activity, and life in the culture and congregation that we encounter the neighbors whom God wants us to love and serve.[6]

Seeing parenting as a vocation changes parents. It changes us to see our children as the neighbor God wants us to love and serve. And it changes us to see ourselves as the means God would use to care for our children—especially as we discover how much we must sacrifice as we're shaped to be more like Christ.

Seeing parenting as a vocation also changes the relationship between parents and the local church. It pushes those who would seek to serve parents beyond just addressing felt needs with a grab bag of this and that. Instead of meeting parents where they are and offering Christian advice and help for their existing parenting hopes and concerns, it prioritizes God's intention to transform them into servants of His love—for His purposes in their lives, in the lives of their children, and in the lives of those in the church body and the community who will also be shaped by their vocation as mother or father. This means that parenting isn't just one of many roles in the life of the believer, but is a primary domain for the Christian life, for service, sanctification, evangelism, and discipleship.

This also has a practical application. A church that understands parenting as a vocation will prioritize "equipping the saints" through teaching, strengthening, and encouraging parents in their vocation. A church will not bear responsibility to do that which parents are primarily called to do themselves. And this likely means the church will purposefully limit its overall activities in order to preserve time for families to be together. Additionally, churches that are encouraging and supporting parents in their vocation will look to those maturing families as a means of evangelism toward other families who don't know

Christ, and as a means of practical support to serve other families who are challenged in their vocation by death, divorce, and other disruptions.

The Means of Grace

Of the ways that the local church can help men and women live out the vocation of parenting, the first priority should be to encourage them to avail themselves of what is known as "the means of grace." Theologian John Frame describes the means of grace as "certain channels by which God gives spiritual power to his church."[7] He categorizes the Christian means of grace under the three headings of the Word, fellowship, and prayer.

In his book *Salvation Belongs to the Lord*, Frame writes:

> Except for the second, we can find those resources either privately or publicly. The second, fellowship, is by definition public. But we can receive the Word either by individual Bible study or through the public preaching and teaching of the church. And we can pray, of course, either privately or publicly. In our private use of the means of grace, we come to God as members of the church, the body of Christ. Apart from Christ, our Bible study and prayer will not help us. Indeed, we need other members of the church to

help us understand the Bible and to teach us how to pray.[8]

In our practical focus on targeted events, programs, and resources, we can overlook—both as parents and those seeking to minister to parents—the spiritual power God has provided already through the means of His Word, fellowship, and prayer. This, in fact, was the focus of the church from the beginning, where we see in Acts 2:42 that after the outpouring of the Holy Spirit, the believers "devoted themselves to the apostles' teaching, to the fellowship, to the breaking of bread, and to the prayers."

Let's consider how the Word, fellowship, and prayer each shape men and women in their vocation as parents and how they can be prioritized for parents in the local church.

The Word

Considering all the advice, influence, and expectations parents face from extended family, friends, neighbors, social media, education, and popular culture, the greatest need parents have is revelation. They need the revelation of creation, the Fall, and redemption in Jesus Christ. They need the gospel to transform them from their former way of life in the world into the fullness of new life revealed in Christ—and that includes renewal from the world's way of parenting.

As John Frame explains, "We can receive the Word either by individual Bible study or through the public preaching and teaching of the church."[9] Parents need the Word at home and in their local church. Parents grow in the vocation of parenting through their commitment to the Word through the means of personal Bible study. And through their vocation of parenting, they serve their children by reading and applying the Bible as a family. It's critical that parents avail themselves of the grace of God's Word at home, but it's also critical that they avail themselves of public preaching and teaching. In recounting how the priests presented the law to the returning exiles in Israel, Nehemiah 8:8 provides a description of the distinctive role of the minister of God's Word: "They read out of the book of the law of God, translating and giving the meaning so that the people could understood what was read."

The best parenting ministry a local church can provide is clear preaching and teaching of the Word from the full counsel of Scripture so that the people can understand the text and apply it to all of life. As a result, the most significant way that parents can avail themselves of the parenting ministry of a church is to lead in taking their family to regular worship—not giving precedence to anything else. And more than just making it to church, they should be active listeners who take notes and follow along closely in the passage being exposited. In this way, parents lead their family in being like the Israelites described in Nehemiah 8:3 where it says, "All the people listened attentively to the book of the law."

Pastors who preach the full counsel of Scripture will provide parents with all they need "for life and godliness" (2 Pet. 1:3). They can do that clearly when they preach faithfully from parenting texts such as Ephesians 6:1–3 or Deuteronomy 6:4–9, but pastors can provide vital parenting ministry even when they aren't preaching on a text that is specifically directed to parents, which will be most of the time. Pastors who are careful in their application of a text will recognize that parenting is one of the primary vocations in their congregation and they won't leave home life exempt from the implications of the passage.

Even if their pastor doesn't give a specific family application, parents can develop the discipline of connecting the dots themselves. They can consider the truths, warnings, and encouragements of each message and ask, "How does this convict and guide me at home, at the dinner table, in the minivan, on the sidelines of a game, or at bedtime?"

The teaching ministry of a church should be the place where men and women look for deeper and more topically focused study of the Word. That's where a church can provide a more focused study on what the Bible teaches parents specifically and can equip them to disciple their children. For example, the most helpful biblical teaching on parenting that we've participated in was the Sunday school series our church led over a couple of months that they adapted from a seminar from Capitol Hill Baptist Church in Washington, DC, (available online). Parents should avail themselves of Sunday schools, midweek services, retreats, or other teaching sessions churches provide that focus on biblical principles for parenting and that help them fruitfully live out their parenting vocation.

Fellowship

The work, the demands, the questions, and the anxieties that are common to parents should show us that we can't make it on our own. We need the input, encouragement, counsel, and example of other people. That motivation is often a primary reason parents will go to church or participate in a range of church activities. And the goal of facilitating fellowship between parents is the impetus behind many of the parenting programs and events churches initiate.

But exactly what kind of fellowship do parents most need and how can churches best serve parents with the fellowship that God intends the church to provide as a means of His grace? Answering those questions requires us to think of fellowship distinctively from the culture of social interaction around us and even from the Christian subculture that often marks our churches.

People in all places and all time have gathered together at some level for social interaction. Today, however, sociologists observe that our social interactions are a mile wide and an inch deep because of the distraction of technological devices that tether us elsewhere. They also observe how social groupings are now often focused narrowly around tribes of people who share economic, ideological, and generational ties and have little contact with those outside of their tribe.

Parents can find social interaction in a variety of settings, but what they really need is the fellowship of other men and women who have been redeemed—people who once walked in darkness, but now walk in light. And that means they need more than a Christian subculture built around tradition, community values, moralism, or any other shared traits outside of Christ crucified and resurrected. In a highly segmented country, the fellowship of believers whom Christ reconciles to Himself and each other should cross all lines of income, race, age, and education level.

That's the ongoing fulfillment of the prayer Jesus prayed with His disciples the night before He was crucified:

> "I pray not only for these, but also for those who believe in me through their word. May they all be one, as you, Father, are in me and I am in you. May they also be in us, so that the world may believe you sent me. I have given them the glory you have given me, so that they may be one as we are one. I am in them and you are in me, so that they may be made completely one, that the world may know you have sent me and have loved them as you have loved me." (John 17:20–23)

That which brings brothers and sisters together in Christ and the reality of what's at stake in our gathering, makes true Christian fellowship radically different from the social interaction we know from any other setting—including much of our traditional Christian subcultures. "The *koinonia*—Greek for commonality, partnership, fellowship—that the first Christians shared wasn't anchored in a common love for pizza, pop, and a nice clean evening of fun among the fellow churchified," writes David Mathis in his book *The Habits of Grace*.[10] He continues:

> Its essence was in their common Christ, and their common life-or-death mission together in his summons to take the faith worldwide in the face of impending persecution. Rightly did Tolkien call his nine "the Fellowship of the Ring." This is no chummy hobnob with apps and drinks and a game on the tube. It is an all-in, life-or-death collective venture in the face of great evil and overwhelming opposition.[11]

This should guide any effort churches make to encourage fellowship among parents. Parents need the fellowship of brothers and sisters in Christ who aren't wasting time trying to keep up appearances of a model family trapped in behavior and reputation management, but who are instead walking in grace—repenting of sin and putting on new life in Christ. They also need more than superficial interactions. Christian fellowship means living out the "one anothers"—loving one another, serving one another, bearing one another's burdens, sharpening one another, and more.

Living out the "one anothers" should mark the fellowship of the local church as men and women gather to worship together with the reading of Scripture, singing, prayer, preaching, and communion. As Paul wrote to the Colossians, "Let the word of Christ dwell richly among you, in all wisdom teaching and admonishing one another through psalms, hymns, and spiritual songs, singing to God with gratitude in your hearts" (Col. 3:16).

Weekly worship is the primary fellowship churches should prioritize for parents. Within that general fellowship, however, parents also need small group settings where they can focus with other church members on their commitment to one another in concentrated discipleship, prayer, accountability, and support. Specific parenting events and programs can offer further elements of fellowship around their vocation as parents, but shouldn't be seen as sufficient outside of their larger fellowship in the body of believers.

To avail themselves of fellowship as a means of grace, parents should join a church and make a commitment to other believers. They should make themselves available and accountable to a small group. And they should also seek the discipleship described in Titus 2:1–8 where older men are called to disciple younger men and older women are called to disciple younger women. These intergenerational relationships in the body are one of the primary means by which God gives parents the example and encouragement they need to live out the vocation of parenting.

Prayer

Few things reveal our inadequacy like being a parent. The responsibility of providing for, protecting, and guiding a dependent child can routinely push us to the limits of our abilities and understanding. For this reason, being a parent can prompt men and women to pray like they never have. But those prayers may not rise above the George Bailey level. In *It's a Wonderful Life,* George Bailey is driven to prayer when he reaches the end of his rope. "Dear Father in heaven, I'm not a praying man," he says, "but if You're up there and You can hear me . . . show me the way . . . show me the way."[12]

Men and women who pray this way show their desperation, but don't realize how utterly dependent they actually are every day of their lives. Parents will not recognize their dependence on prayer until they grasp the truth of what Jesus told His disciples the night before He was crucified. "You can do nothing without me" (John 15:5b). And parents will not know the depths of Christ's generous offer in prayer until they trust what He says next. "If you remain in me and my words remain in you, ask whatever you want and it will be done for you" (John 15:7).

"Prayer is the very heart of the Christian life," writes David Mathis. "Not only is it obedience to God's counsel, but it is a vital means of our receiving his ongoing grace for our spiritual survival and thriving."[13]

Prayer is vital for men and women to survive and thrive in the vocation of parenting. Their means to serve their children in love comes from daily going to their heavenly Father in praise and worship, in confession of sin, in thanksgiving for all His goodness, and with all their requests—from the seemingly mundane to the critical. And in their vocation of parenting, they serve their children by praying with them—at prayers for meals, but also at the beginning of the day, at bedtime, and at other opportunities in between.

Parents especially serve their children by praying for them. In fact, they see how critical their prayers are for their children when they realize that ultimately only God can change their children's hearts. Our prayers are an admission that we are truly dependent on God to accomplish the goal of our parenting—that our children would trust and follow Christ from the heart.

It is critical that parents avail themselves of the grace of prayer at home, but it is also critical that they avail themselves of corporate prayer. "Prayer is for all of life, and especially for our life together in community," writes Mathis. "When we follow the lead of the Scriptures, we not only practice prayer in private, but take its spirit of dependence and trust into the rest of the day, and into times of focused prayer together with fellow believers."[14]

A church serves parents through its commitment to corporate prayer and to careful prayer about the ministry efforts to which it commits.

Corporate prayer—the time of praise, confession, thanksgiving, and requests—can often include a petition to God for strength, wisdom, and grace for parents to serve their children in love. But corporate prayer serves parents even if their needs aren't specifically mentioned because of the way group prayer shapes individual prayer. "The more earnestly we pray in solitude, the more powerfully we will pray in a group," says John Piper. "And the more intense the prayer of the group, the more we will be helped to go hard after God in private."[15] Parents should avail themselves of public prayer times like these that shape their private prayer while also praying earnestly alone that they may pray more boldly with others.

Churches should prioritize corporate prayer as an essential part of the weekly worship service while also providing additional times for extended prayer. We commend the corporate prayer commitment in our local church. There, the church sets aside nearly five minutes on Sunday morning to, as they describe it, "1) rejoice in who God is and all that He's done in Christ, 2) confess our need of His grace, 3) and bring our requests to Him."[16] On Wednesday nights, the church sets aside close to thirty minutes to pray for missions, evangelism, the sick, and families (including engaged couples, expectant and adopting parents, and couples suffering from infertility). At small group gatherings, men and women divide for focused prayer time that often includes praying over specific challenges and needs they face as moms and dads. Prayer is also central in Sunday school, retreats, and other special gatherings.

Prayer is critical to guiding what ministry efforts churches take on and how those efforts proceed. A church should make no ministry commitment without much prayerful consideration and then regular prayer for fruitfulness. "While you join in helping us by your prayers," Paul wrote to the Corinthians. "Then many will give thanks on our behalf for the gift that came to us through the prayers of many" (2 Cor. 1:11). Paul routinely demonstrated his dependence on prayer for fruitful ministry.

Church leaders seeking to serve parents faithfully should pray first and foremost that their church will prioritize ministry of the Word, prayer, and fellowship that encourages and guides men and women to love and serve in their vocation as parents. Secondarily, church leaders should pray about what focused teaching they could provide on biblical parenting and what setting would serve the parents in their church best. Beyond those commitments, church leaders should pray about what efforts may still be needed in which they could bring the means of teaching, prayer, and fellowship together with the goal of encouraging and guiding parents in their vocation (especially those who may be challenged in their vocation by death, divorce, or other disruptions). They should also pray earnestly about how they can guide families who are growing in grace to reach those families who don't know Christ and to serve those needing practical support and care.

Lead at Home

The second commitment doesn't need as much explanation, but it's essential for how churches serve parents. The simple idea is that anyone seeking to minister to parents should first lead faithfully in his own home and then serve pastorally like a loving, committed parent.

This is drawn from 1 Thessalonians 2 where the apostle Paul describes his ministry to the family of God as serving in a manner expected of mothers and fathers. "We were gentle among you, as a nurse nurtures her own children," Paul writes in verse 7. "We cared so much for you that we were pleased to share with you not only the gospel of God but also our own lives" (v. 8). Paul goes on in verses 10–12 to write:

> You are witnesses, and so is God, of how devoutly,
> righteously, and blamelessly we conducted ourselves
> with you believers. As you know, like a father with
> his own children, we encouraged, comforted, and

implored each one of you to live worthy of God, who calls you into his own kingdom and glory.

The primary point is not about parenting, it's about ministry, but this passage guides both. To demonstrate his care in ministry, Paul pointed to examples his readers would understand and admire in a father or mother. Ministers of the gospel should look to Paul's model of proclaiming the truth, leading by example, and loving warmly—but they shouldn't miss the expectation implied for the kind of father they should be in their own home.

Children need the kind of affection, example, and exhortation that Paul references—especially for their discipleship. The primary means of discipleship parents have in the home are reading and applying Scripture; living as consistent examples of people who love the Jesus they're speaking about by following Him faithfully and depending on His mercy as they repent of sin; and showing an affectionate, committed love that pervades it all.

"The parental relationship teaches through imitation and instruction," says Jeremy Pierre, a professor of biblical counseling at The Southern Baptist Theological Seminary. "There's great power in consistency when a message and a life line up." He explains that parents should "demonstrate personal commitment to, and enjoyment, of the gospel of Jesus Christ in front of children while instructing them carefully in it."[17]

A church's ability to minister to parents begins with their leaders' commitment in their own homes, and then depends on a pastoral commitment to proclaiming the truth, loving warmly, and being an example with their lives. Tactics are lifeless without example, exhortation, and affection. Fruitful ministry depends on pastors being faithful to the Word, loving with Christ's love, and walking out their new life in Christ for others to see.

Churches can be fruitful in their ministry to parents, when 1) pastors, who are faithful in affection, example, and exhortation at home and in their ministry in the church, 2) prioritize serving parents with faithful preaching and teaching of the Word, fellowship, and corporate prayer, 3) so that parents can avail themselves of the means of grace and grow in their vocation as parents, serving their children in love, and 4) growing in their ministry within the body as a witness to families that don't know Christ and as a support for those who are challenged in their parenting vocation by death, divorce, and other disruptions.

You may be a pastor seeking to serve parents who are prone to leave your church property and sneak in a Starbucks date, or you may be those parents who have availed themselves of free babysitting, but little else. Our prayer is that both pastors and parents reading this will love more and more the means of grace God has provided to us in our homes and in the local church for our growth in serving our children in love.

Discussion Questions

. . . .

1. How does the doctrine of vocation change how we see our work as parents?
2. How does faithful preaching of the Word serve parents?
3. How can fellowship be a means of God's grace for parents?
4. How can the public prayer at church shape a parent's private prayer at home?

CHAPTER

5

What Does the Culture Say?

David E. Prince

"I CANNOT BELIEVE THAT YOU WOULD DO THAT!"

Years ago, my wife, Judi, and I had one of those "aha moments." It was something we should have realized earlier, but for some reason we had missed it. We suddenly recognized that we had been responding to our children's sin in a way that rendered them Pharisees-in-training.

We were reflexively parroting familiar cultural language that was pushing our children in the opposite direction of where we wished for them to go. It was very common for us to respond to our children's sin by saying, "We cannot believe that you would do that! We are not people who do those kinds of things." As parents who embrace an evangelical understanding of sin and the universality of human depravity, the language we so frequently used betrayed our stated conviction.

Our words communicated that we expected good kids and that we were stunned at any behavior that showed they were not good kids. The implication was that they were expected to be *good kids* because we were a *good family*. We were aware of the dangers associated with a very permissive parenting style. We had seen the ramifications of such in our worldly culture. Yet, we did not recognize that there was equal danger with strict parenting if it marginalized the gospel.

The reality is that the gospel can be obscured in both strict and permissive models of parenting.

We knew Romans 3:23, "For all have sinned and fall short of the glory of God" and quoted it often when sharing the gospel of Jesus Christ. But functionally, the culture our words were creating in our home tacitly implied we were exempt from the depravity and power of sin. I am not exactly sure when it happened, but at some point Judi and I decided we needed to change our language in order to be faithful gospel witnesses in our own home. We sought to banish the language, "We cannot believe you would do that! We are not people who do those kinds of things!"

We replaced it with, "I am not at all surprised you would sin in this way. I have sinned in similar ways. This is a good opportunity to remember that you do not simply sin but that you are a sinner." The first approach was gospel-less. The second approach is "in step with the truth of the gospel" (Gal. 2:14 ESV).

Worldly Words

The way we had been responding to sin focused on how our child was letting us down. It was about his or her failure to live up to the family standard of righteousness. The new approach puts the focus on God. It points toward His standard of righteousness and paves the way for clarity about the good news of salvation. It presents a strategic opportunity for the Christian parent to say something like, "I am a sinner too, but I have been forgiven of my sins by faith in Jesus Christ, and I am praying that the discipline you receive will remind you that sin has consequences and that you, too, will seek forgiveness in Jesus Christ."

Framing discipline in an anti-gospel way places children on a performance treadmill. Their lives are based on meeting your expectations. And the only outcome of that approach is defeat and despair. Conviction of sin will bring no joy. It will only bring shame because they will reason, "I have failed my parents who thought I was a good person. Now, they know I am not a good person because I have these thoughts and act this way. I must be worthless." Constant accusation without the gospel is hellish, not holy.

As Christian parents, we need to make sure our words match our doctrine when we discipline our children. Every instance of parental discipline is a strategic opportunity to expose our children's true identity (and ours too)—sinners who need a Savior. That is what is so powerful about gospel-focused discipline. When a parent clarifies the sin, points to the gospel, administers the discipline, and then embraces the child joyfully and forgivingly by declaring, "I love you no matter what!" the child gets a small taste of the glorious and absolute freedom offered in the gospel (Gal. 5:1).

Christian parents often have good intentions. But so often, we fall into the trap of embracing the culture's expectations for our children's lives, so we raise our kids based on the same things non-Christian parents value rather than anything distinctively Christian. We are called to love God by loving our children, but too often we love the vision of raising (culturally) successful children. Seeing a child meet cultural expectations can easily become the way parents validate themselves. Parents who base parenting decisions on other people's perception of them and their family's social standing are tragically treating their children like props in a public relations campaign. Faithful, cruciform, Christian parenting demands an intentional commitment to take every parenting thought captive to obey Christ and embrace distinctively Christian, gospel-focused aspirations.

Worldliness Comes with Good Manners

In Ephesians, Paul declares that the triune God is at work in heaven and on earth summing up all things in Christ (1:10). Like all things, Christian parenting is to be summed up in Christ. This means that there is a Christ-centered, gospel-saturated, and cruciform distinctness to faithful Christian parenting. Our parenting must create a culture in our home where the gospel is becoming more intelligible, or we will inevitably design a culture where the gospel is becoming unintelligible. Failure to cultivate a gospel-filled home will yield children who are saturated in the wisdom of the world.

Worldliness is not a word that Christians use much anymore. There is a sense in which avoiding the word can be beneficial because many Christians have defined worldliness in a way that is at odds with the biblical definition. We often think of worldliness only in terms of moral behavior. People with the right behavior are the good guys and inherently morally superior. People with the wrong behavior are the bad guys and inherently morally inferior. And of course, we want our children to be the good guys, the morally superior ones. But in 1 and 2 Corinthians, Paul uses the term *worldliness* in a way that is at odds with this conception. According to Paul, there are those who live based on the word of the cross, which is the wisdom of God, and there are those who trust the wisdom of the world, which is focused on personal strength, gifts, and abilities. Those determined to view the world through the lens of Christ crucified have their identity in Christ and His Kingdom. Those who live based on the wisdom of the world focus on self-interest and self-satisfaction and find their identity in self-referential achievement and accomplishment.

The dividing line between the Christian and the world is not found in moral superiority, but a crucified Messiah. We are all guilty sinners in need of a Savior. Consequently, we cannot discuss our child's behavior on the world's terms and simply tack Christianity on as an addendum to the discussion.

The Christian parent's goal is not good kids—it is gospel kids. The Christian parent's goal in discipline is not low-maintenance, well-mannered children, but gospel proclamation.

According to Paul, worldliness is defining the world outside the lens of the gospel. It comes packaged in both conservative and liberal morality. While worldliness can sometimes come with bad manners, it can easily come with good manners too. Our goal must be to teach our children that the gospel redefines every category in their lives (2 Cor. 10:5). It gives them a new lens through which to see the world.

When the apostle Paul declared, "I decided to know nothing among you except Jesus Christ and him crucified," he was not suggesting that the cross of Christ was the only thought that ever entered his mind, nor was he saying that he tacked on some commentary about Jesus' death to every dialogue (1 Cor. 2:2). Paul was contending that the power and wisdom of God on display in the crucifixion and resurrection of Christ served as the only proper frame of reference for every single thought.

So how does a Christian whose life is committed to following Jesus think about and react to sin in the life of their children? The pattern begins with confronting the child about their sin. Following this, the parent explains to the child that he or she is praying that God will use the discipline to teach the child that they need to ask forgiveness for their sin. Gospel-focused parents teach their children that sin is a heart problem. Teach that sin has consequences and point to the gospel as the only ultimate answer.

An Image-Centered Parenting Plan—Gospel Not Included

Intentional, cruciform, Christian parenting is not marked by self-pity. Each time a child's sin is uncovered and exposed, it provides a unique gospel opportunity. Parents must embrace their God-given responsibility as stewards of the gospel in their children's lives (Eph. 6:1–4). It would be a nightmare, not a blessing, if children were so adept at concealing sin that their parents never caught them in a sinful deed. It is only when the gospel has been eclipsed in our thinking that we wish we did not have to deal with our children's sin. Only those who see and confess their sin can ever cry out, "God, have mercy on me, a sinner!" (Luke 18:13). When Christian parents communicate that the real issue is our embarrassment that our children would do such a thing, we are implicitly endorsing the attitude of the Pharisee who said, "God, I thank you that I am not like other people" (Luke 18:11). Such an approach does not constitute shepherding a child's heart but rather managing an image by focusing on externals.

In some Christian circles it is not uncommon for parents to dismiss their permissive parenting as loving or showing grace. Such language fails to comport with a biblical understanding of gospel love and grace. The Scripture describes parents who do not exercise authority and discipline as a demonstration of hatred rather than love (Prov. 13:24). The gospel is not God looking the other way when we sin and letting us off the hook. Rather, the gospel declares that, on the cross, Jesus satisfied the wrath of God for sinners who put their faith in Him. Authority without love leads to authority being despised, and love without authority makes love unintelligible. The typical cultural approach to parenting is to be generally permissive while strictly enforcing anything that is public and could harm the family image. Such an approach is a fast-track to pharisaism and must be rejected by parents who desire their child training and nurturing to be distinctly Christian.

Any child-centric approach to parenting is an unspiritual discipline that inevitably gravitates toward Pharisee cultivation—image control. The general cultural ethos is that good parents put their child first in all things, first in material provisions, first in time commitments, and they attempt to make their child's path as easy as possible. Often, this includes neglecting the most important gift that parents provide their children, which is a home based on a loving, gospel-centered marriage as a first priority. A loving marriage is foundational for faithful Christian parenting because God's design for marriage is for it to serve as a living picture of Christ and the church (Eph. 5:32). The relationship between husband and wife is the closest and most sacred on earth, and it must be primary if the gospel is the priority in raising your child. Yet, too many Christian families are guilty of imitating a child-centered idolatry they have seen in the larger culture. Parents, who center their lives on their children to the neglect of Jesus Christ and their marriage relationship, are unwittingly teaching them a pattern of narcissistic discontentment.

Be Nice, Be Happy, and Be Safe—An Anti-Christ Parenting Manifesto

It seems the modern American parenting manifesto is: Be nice, be happy, and be safe—no matter what. The problem is that none of those assertions represent distinctly Christian values.

In 2005, Christian Smith and researchers at The National Study of Youth and Religion at the University of North Carolina at Chapel Hill took a close look at the religious beliefs of churched American teenagers. They found a faith they described as "Moralistic Therapeutic Deism," which can be summarized as a belief in a God who exists if needed; and who wants to help people be nice, happy, safe; and if they are, they will go to heaven when they die. I fear that this is a theological worldview these teenagers learned by observing what their parents really valued and prioritized on a daily basis.

Out of an obsession to keep children happy, many parents act like victims who must provide children with every wish or desire. I recently heard a father explaining to another parent, "I didn't want to get her an iPhone yet, but I had to because every child in her class has one. I don't want her to be considered weird." His daughter was eight years old.

Children who grow up getting everything they desire most often live very unhappy lives. Parents, who provide their children with twenty-four-hours-a-day, unmonitored access to the

Internet—including the use of smart phones and computers in the bedroom—in an effort not to restrict their freedom, are sentencing their children to a life of bondage. Few things are more pitiful than a young person who was reared in an environment of self-indulgent freedom that resulted in enslavement to pornography.

Jesus' declaration, "If anyone wants to follow after me, let him deny himself, take up his cross daily, and follow me" (Luke 9:23), means that teaching self-denial is an important part of cruciform parenting.

Of all of the names people called Jesus in the Bible, never once was He referred to as nice or safe. Jesus was described as one who speaks with authority, a madman, a glutton, a blasphemer, a sinner, and as one who acted by demonic power. Jesus did not cozy up comfortably with the wisdom of the world, but rather turned the wisdom of the world upside down.

In an age of helicopter parenting, Christian parents should know better than to constantly hover over their children in an attempt to mitigate potential risks and mistakes. Living life involves inevitable risks, and Christian parents must teach their children to take self-sacrificial, calculated risks for the glory of Christ and the good of others.

Safety is far less important than Christ-exalting bravery and courage. Parents must intentionally train their children toward both physical and moral courage. According to biblical wisdom, laziness is not just a physical problem. Laziness is a spiritual one and it represents a life of wickedness and folly. The mother or father who is satisfied with having a nice child who makes good grades but sleeps in until noon and does very little in the way of sacrificially serving the family and others is a parenting fool (Prov. 6:6–11; 21:25; 26:13–16). We live in a superficial age that exalts intentional underachievement with participation trophies and "everyone is a winner" slogans. Christian parents should be defying the spirit of the age by teaching children cruciform ambition, "So, whether you eat or drink, or whatever you do, do everything for the glory of God" (1 Cor. 10:31).

In parenting seminars, I will frequently ask parents to estimate how many times in a given year that they tell their children to be careful and safe. Once they settle on an estimated number in their mind, I ask also them to estimate how many times in a year they challenge their children to be courageous, brave, or to take an action for the sake of someone else that might put them in harm's way. The response is almost always the same; they constantly tell their kids to be careful and safe, and rarely ever tell them to be self-sacrificially courageous and brave. There are enormous deleterious effects in raising a generation of people who believe that there is nothing more important than their personal comfort and safety.

Most parents are aghast by the thought of teaching their children that there are times they should put themselves in harm's way. Many consider it inherently reckless. But, the distinction between recklessness and courage is actually easy to discern. Recklessness is motivated by no higher purpose than the danger itself, whereas courageousness is self-sacrificial for a higher, others-centered purpose. Courage is not the absence of fear; it is acting on the premise that there is something more important than fear. Or as the great American theologian John Wayne put it, "Courage is being scared to death, but saddling up anyway," and I would add, "saddling up for the self-sacrificial good of others."

Christian parents ought to make courage and bravery a major part of the family vocabulary. Read and talk about courageous people in history. When your child does something that demands courage, celebrate it with a special meal or reward. Train toward courage. If your child does not naturally talk to people, assign them to initiate a conversation with five people at church each week and hold them accountable to do it. At the end of the week, ask each family member to share something they did that required bravery. I love to hear about things my children did not want to do, but did anyway, because they knew it was right and helpful to someone else.

To live as if nothing is more important than personal safety is to live an empty, selfish, and ultimately dissatisfying life. That kind of entitlement mentality only leads to self-referential pride and discontentment. Jesus is our model and embodiment of true self-sacrificial courage. His meekness was not weakness. His humility was not moral feebleness. And His courage was costly. Christian parents must teach children that one can be both safe and large-hearted. We often complain about our selfish culture while at the same time teaching our children that nothing is as important as them and their safety. We dream about our children leading noble and courageous lives while we train them daily toward cowardice.

I fear that in the name of nice, happy, safe children many Christian families are practically abandoning "the faith that was delivered to the saints once for all" (Jude 3). Affirming the gospel message with our lips, while parenting on a daily basis as if it is not true, will have disastrous consequences. Adults who believe life is about being nice, happy, and safe do not joyfully commit their lives to take the gospel to the ends of the earth (Acts 5:41). In fact, when they hear about someone self-sacrificially suffering for the advance of the gospel, they may woefully respond, "I cannot believe that you would do that!"

Suggestions for Combating the Parenting Wisdom of the World with Gospel Intentionality

A parent who is not intentional in their child-rearing is functioning as a really attached sitter. The child-sitter is not attempting to cultivate anything in the lives of the children they are watching. The sitter simply wants the kids to enjoy the time and avoid any crisis or major difficulty. The sitter merely wants to survive the time with the children, not thrive.

A recent study on the origins of narcissism in children concluded, "narcissism in children is cultivated by parental overvaluation: parents believing their child to be more special and more entitled than others."[18] The summary of the study further explains, "children seem to acquire narcissism, in part, by internalizing parents' inflated views of them." Unfortunately, the "you are so special, so smart, so beautiful, so talented, so gifted—you can do anything you want to do and be anything you want to be" mantra is often believed, and our children suffer because of it.

Avoid Counterproductive Praise

The study dovetails with *New York Times* best seller *Nurture Shock: New Thinking about Children* by Po Bronson and Ashley Merryman. Their research concluded that heaping praise on children detached from achievement in an effort to boost their self-esteem is counterproductive. They assert that the result of this "self-esteem above all else" approach to parenting has produced a generation of American young adults who feel better about themselves though they achieve less and fear challenges. Every Christian parent ought to know there are grave implications for nurturing children with this type of self-oriented flattery.

Above all people, Christian parents who understand the gospel of Christ should know that a smiley-faced sentimental approach to child-rearing is an ineffective placebo for preparing their children for the spiritual war that is life. Over-praising children detached from achievement encourages them to live based on a false image of self and engenders fear that they might be exposed as not so special, smart, talented, beautiful, or gifted. Such parenting makes children inordinately self-conscious and frequently discontent.

Help Make the Gospel Intelligible

Above all else, a Christian parent's job is to create categories in their children's daily lives that help make the gospel intelligible as they prepare them for adulthood. Foundational to a Christian worldview is the truth: "God resists the proud but gives grace to the humble" (James 4:6; 1 Pet. 5:5). Parents must exercise authority over their children, not for their own sake, but for their children's sake. Teaching your children to live under appropriate authority is a gift that leads to contentment. A gospel-centered approach to parenting that cultivates a biblical worldview will not abandon honest conversation about the child's strengths (where appropriate praise is vital) and weaknesses.

This gospel-centered approach also means parents should be honest with their children about their own faults as parents and followers of Jesus. Christian parents must not try to portray themselves as perfect because their goal is to point their children to a Savior who alone is perfect. When a parent apologizes to a child because they lost their temper, or sinned against the child in some way, they are displaying Christian strength, not weakness, because their goal is to point their child to the gospel. No parent can teach their children that Jesus is Lord while they are at the same time pretending that they are Lord.

Practical Suggestions

Below are some simple suggestions on how to raise non-narcissistic children who have been taught the value of humility, submission, and hard work. I consider these suggestions to be sanctified, Christian common sense.

1. **Tell your children the truth.** No really, tell them the truth. Do not tell them the empty delusional clichés like, "If you believe it, you can achieve it." If they are not very good at something say, "You are not very good at _____, so here is how you can work hard to get better, and if you don't get better, here is how you can serve others or help your team." After all, no one is the best at everything, but they can strive to be their best at what they do and value their contribution in the role they play. Sounds a lot like Paul's description of life in the church (1 Cor. 12).

2. **Say "no" often and mean it.** Saying "no" is a gift; maturity and freedom cannot take place without it, and

it also makes it meaningful when you say "yes." A parent who rarely says "no" to his or her children or only does so apologetically is cultivating an entitlement mentality and setting them up for failure as adults. Humbly hearing "no" from someone in authority and resourcefully pressing ahead with eagerness is a foundational life skill, and such ought to be obvious to a people who declare, "Jesus is Lord."

3. **Always support the coach's and teacher's decisions (even if they are wrong).** It is easy to react to questions about playing time or issues in the classroom by giving all priority to the child's temporal feelings. It may be that your child is better than the kid who is starting in front of him or her or that the assignment from the teacher is arbitrary. So what? The real question is how he or she responds to the situation. Tell them, "Most coaches want to win, and if they thought you gave them the best opportunity to win, they would be playing you. Keep working." Teach them that it is not the job of the teacher to adjust to them; it is their job to adjust to the teacher. The teacher is the authority in the room, not your child. This is great life preparation. Teach them to live for God's glory.

4. **Require that they use honorific titles.** Doing so cultivates a basic respect for authority and a willingness to recognize hierarchal structures and roles that God has wisely ordained. Demanding your children use Mister, Miss(es), Doctor, Officer, President, Governor, and so

forth is a consistent theology lesson. Few things are more detrimental to shaping a biblical worldview than a child walking up to an older man and saying, "Hey, Bob." Or, as is often the case in my conservative evangelical circles, children speak of politicians with whom they disagree with a sneering disrespect, and parents approve because they disagree with the politician's positions. Do we really want to teach our children that they do not have to show respect for those in authority because they disagree? What about when they disagree with you?

I hope these simple suggestions will provide a helpful gospel trajectory. If Christian parents desire to hear their children say, "Jesus is Lord" (1 Cor. 12:3), take up their cross and follow Him (Luke 9:23), and to count others as more important than themselves (Phil. 2:3), then the empty, self-referential, flattery model of parenting must be abandoned in favor of a cruciform, gospel-shaped model.

Conclusion: More Gospel Intentionality and Less Cultural Manipulation

A parent who wants to become more gospel-focused must abandon culturally driven manipulation. I was counseling a man whose children were in rebellion and his marriage was in trouble. I asked him, "What makes a good father?" He did not hesitate to respond saying, "Providing needs and wants for your children financially, giving them opportunities to do the things they want, and paying for college." According to him, that was a complete summary of what it meant to be a good father. Of course, the only thing on his list that was biblically justifiable was providing for the needs (not wants) of his children financially. Everything else was simply what the culture said good dads should do for their children.

I told him that his priorities were not biblical and he thought that was one of the strangest things he'd ever heard. I told him that I wanted my children to love and serve Christ and His church above all else. I told him that I make sure my children know that I would rather them be poor and love Jesus than wealthy and not love Jesus. His marriage difficulties and problems with his children were a result of his misplaced priorities. Our children know what we truly value and prioritize. If we communicate to them that we believe nothing is more important than education or career success, we should not act surprised if they order their lives in that way. After years of counseling, I can assure you that education and career success do not necessarily result in Christian joy and satisfaction.

My oldest son is an excellent student. He was valedictorian of his high school class and received a large academic scholarship for college. He decided to pursue a degree in education. Sadly, when people asked what he was studying, they often responded, "You could be anything you want to be. Why would you go into education? Don't you know that educators don't make very much money?" He was barraged with those kinds of comments from Christians, just as often as from non-Christians. He once said, "Mom and Dad, I just want to thank you for not treating me like a failure if I don't pursue a higher-paying career." He added, "Many of my classmates' parents are pressuring them to choose a career based on potential future income too." We assured him that being a teacher to the glory of Christ sounded great to us.

Intentionally focusing on Jesus and His gospel in parenting will cause other concerns to be displaced as priorities. This is almost a complete reversal of the way the task of parenting is approached in our culture. The common cultural model is for parents to be permissive on a daily basis and hands-off as far as cultivating their child's daily thought patterns and worldview. This is coupled with becoming heavy-handed and manipulative in pushing their children toward cultural expectations when it comes to big decisions about college, career, and life. In contrast, parents who do the hard work of providing godly discipline, biblical character formation, and shepherding their children's heart, will also have a different view when it's time for their children to leave home and declare Jesus' lordship with their lives. After all, our parenting priority is not that our children become trophies (idols) that testify to our parenting skill but that they become arrows we expectantly release for God and His glory.

Discussion Questions

• • • • • • • • • • • • • • •

1. How does framing discipline in an anti-gospel way place children on performance treadmills? In discipline, how do we make sure our words match our doctrine? Why is it important to do this?

2. What is the difference between a parent and a sitter? How can the obsession to make children "happy" actually contribute to lifelong bondage?

3. Why should parents take an active role in cultivating their children's thought patterns and worldview? How is this contrary to the "hands-off" model encouraged by the culture?

4. In light of the trends in our culture, why is it important to raise non-narcissistic children? How do we teach them the values of humility, submission, and work?

ADDITIONAL READING

Shepherding a Child's Heart by Tedd Tripp

Missional Motherhood by Gloria Furman

Gospel-Powered Parenting: How the Gospel Shapes and Transforms Parenting by William Farley

Age of Opportunity: A Biblical Guide to Parenting Teens by Paul Tripp

Common Sense Parenting by Kent and Barbara Hughes

ACKNOWLEDGMENTS

TO THE MANY HANDS INSIDE AND OUTSIDE THE ERLC, WE thank you for your help and assistance on this book. The ERLC team provided joyful encouragement in the planning and execution of this series, and without them, it would never have gotten off the ground. We want to also personally thank Phillip Bethancourt who was a major visionary behind this project. We'd also like to thank Jennifer Lyell and Devin Maddox at B&H, our publisher, for their work in guiding us through this process.

ABOUT THE ERLC

THE ERLC IS DEDICATED TO ENGAGING THE CULTURE WITH the gospel of Jesus Christ and speaking to issues in the public square for the protection of religious liberty and human flourishing. Our vision can be summed up in three words: kingdom, culture, and mission. Since its inception, the ERLC has been defined around a holistic vision of the kingdom of God, leading the culture to change within the church itself and then as the church addresses the world. The ERLC has offices in Washington, DC, and Nashville, Tennessee.

ABOUT THE CONTRIBUTORS

Timothy Paul Jones serves as the C. Edwin Gheens Professor of Christian Family Ministry at The Southern Baptist Theological Seminary in Louisville, Kentucky. He is the husband of Rayann and the father of three daughters. The Jones family serves in children's ministry and community group leadership at the east congregation of Sojourn Community Church.

David E. Prince is married to Judi, and they have eight children. He is the pastor of preaching and vision at Ashland Avenue Baptist Church in Lexington, Kentucky, and assistant professor of Christian preaching at The Southern Baptist Theological Seminary. He is the author of *In the Arena* and *Church with Jesus as the Hero*. He blogs at Prince on Preaching and frequently writes for The Ethics and Religious Liberty Commission, For the Church, and Preaching Today.

Randy Stinson is the senior vice president for Academic Administration and Provost; Basil Manly Jr. Professor of Leadership and Family Ministry at The Southern Baptist Theological Seminary.

Tedd and Margy Tripp, Ted is pastor emeritus of Grace Fellowship Church and author of *Shepherding a Child's Heart,* and Ted's wife Margy is coauthor of *Instructing a Child's Heart.*

Candice and Steve Watters met at Regent University while earning their Master's Degrees in Public Policy. Marrying shortly after graduation, they moved to Colorado to work at Focus on the Family. They founded Boundless.org Webzine for Focus in 1998. Candice served as the *Boundless* editor for four years until leaving in 2002 to be a full-time mom, doing a little freelance writing and editing on the side. Candice is the author of *Get Married: What Women Can Do to Help It Happen.* Together they wrote *Start Your Family: Inspiration for Having Babies.* Steve is the vice president for communications at The Southern Baptist Theological Seminary. They have four children: Harrison, Zoe, Churchill, and Teddy.

NOTES

1. This chapter was developed from my teaching session in Men's Leadership School at the Jeffersontown congregation of Sojourn Community Church on February 24, 2016; some portions of that teaching session were drawn from *Family Ministry Field Guide* (Indianapolis, IN: Wesleyan, 2011) and *Practical Family Ministry* (Nashville, TN: Randall House, 2015).

2. Martin Luther, "Tertia Disputatio: Alia Ratio Iustificandi Hominis Coram Deo," *Quinque Disputationes,* thesis 6.

3. D. L. Moody, *Notes from My Bible* (Chicago, IL: Revell, 1895), 152.

4. Mark Kelly, "LifeWay Research Looks at the Role of Faith in Parenting" (March 24, 2009), http://www.lifeway.com.

5. Gene Edward Veith Jr. and Mary J. Moerbe, *Family Vocation: God's Calling in Marriage, Parenting, and Childhood* (Wheaton, IL: Crossway, 2012), 29.

6. Ibid.

7. John M. Frame, *Salvation Belongs to the Lord* (Phillipsburg, NJ: P&R, 2006), 260–61.

8. Ibid.

9. Ibid.

10. David Mathis, *Habits of Grace: Enjoying Jesus through the Spiritual Disciplines* (Wheaton, IL: Crossway, 2016), 145.

11. Ibid.

12. *It's a Wonderful Life,* "Quotes," Internet Movie Database http://www.imdb.com/title/tt0038650/quotes.

13. David Mathis, "When Prayer Comes out of the Closet," Desiring God, http://www.desiringgod.org/articles/when-prayer-comes -out-of-the-closet.

14. Ibid.

15. John Piper, "Sweet 'Our' of Prayer" message January 4, 1987. Available online at http://www.desiringgod.org/messages/sweet-our-of -prayer.

16. "Sunday Morning Prayer at Clifton Baptist Church" document provided to church members leading in prayer during the morning service.

17. Jeremy Pierre, Lecture in Marriage and Family Counseling course at The Southern Baptist Theological Seminary, November 13, 2012.

18. Ed. Susan T. Fiske, Princeton University, Princeton, NJ, and approved February 12, 2015 (received for review November 7, 2014), "Origins of narcissism in children" in The Proceedings of the National Academy of Sciences in America, accessed http://www.pnas.org/content /112/12/3659.abstract on 10.11.16.